THINGS *to* COME

When Prophecy & Revelation Collide

THINGS *to* COME

When Prophecy & Revelation Collide

Andy Sanders

5 Fold Media
Visit us at www.5foldmedia.com

Dedication

Cathy

You have been the most solid Christian I have ever met in my life. In times of trouble, you have been unwavering. In times of extreme turmoil, you keep going and never look back. You, without question, are the most matured individual I have ever encountered. Your walk with God is obviously not out of happenstance, blessing, or tradition. It is from the depth of your heart and the core of your soul. Thank you for showing me how to truly live a Christ-centered life.

Michael & Joselyn

The two of you are the greatest gifts and blessings anyone could ever have. I am so proud of you both and am honored to be your dad. You have followed your parents everywhere God has asked us to lead you, and you have done it without complaint. God bless you both.

Dad, Mom, and Brother

Thank you for being my biological family. You are the only father, mother, and brother I will ever have. The older I get, the more I miss all of you.

Dave & Gloria

You both have been the greatest in-laws one could ever ask for. Without your unyielding love and acceptance of my life, I would not have made it this far.

Contents

Introduction

L ike every person, we all want to believe that we have lived for the greater good—that our lives have counted for something and our brief time on this earth has made a positive impact on other people. Most individuals that I have been with at the time of their death never really talk about how they wished they could have cleaned their truck more, washed the dishes better, or even worked harder at their former jobs. Quite the opposite is actually true. Every person that I have ever witnessed be summoned to their Maker recalled the moments they were with their family members and emphasized how they wished they could spend just a little more time with them. I have also noticed a big difference between a Christian passing on into eternal glory, and someone who is not born again at the time of their death. I have yet to see a believer cross over into the afterlife scared. Every one of them were sad to say goodbye to their family and friends, but anxiously awaiting the face-to-face encounter with their Creator.

You only live once, my friends, and what you do on this earth from the time you were born until the time you pass can only be determined by you. At the end of this journey, you are ultimately responsible for how you lived on earth, and where you are going to spend eternity. Choose to live morally and do good to as many people around you as possible. Make a mark on society for Jesus.

I started out on the wrong path in life, but by God's sovereign love and divine grace that so radically touched my life, I am free today—

not just here and now, but also in the next life to come. Something that I wish to pass onto you, the reader, is just how much God longs to speak and illustrate His almighty, yet personal presence. He wants to know you! Jesus came to set you free and impart His glorious Spirit into your being. He is not a far and distant God, much the opposite; the Lord is a personal God that longs for mankind more than mankind longs for Him. Be the one who chooses to touch His heart. Become the person who allows others around you to discover more of God simply because God is releasing so much through you.

This is why I have written this book. I want you to discover just how much God wants to speak to you and touch your life. God is looking for people that will pass on His love through a vast supply of creative gifts. Heaven is certainly not lacking in supply and it most definitely isn't running out of new ideas. So don't be shy! Figure out how to lay hold of the promises of God and pass them on to everyone around you.

As for this book and what you are about to read, freedom comes through a process. It is not just your salvation experience, but it is all the paths that God chose for your life that led you up to the time Christ revealed Himself to you. From the moment you opened your heart to Him, your life unfolds much like a story being written daily by the almighty hand of God.

From this perspective, I have chosen to write this book. It has been many years in the making with much research. This particular book has many different short teachings in it. Most of the stories are little nuggets that God has taught me over the past ten years. All are prophetic in nature and toward the end there are some short prophetic fiction stories that I believe are a glimpse of just some of the things that are coming in the future, as wild as they may seem.

This book is not necessarily a devotional, but simply a collection of teachings that are a great tool to stretch your ability to look beyond what you currently see and upward toward the glory of our coming King. Reading this book will require you to see past the pages, and in some cases, deep into the supernatural. Most importantly, always let the Bible be your daily source and guide. The Word of God will change you more than anything else. I encourage you to have your Bible ready with this book, flipping from one verse to the next, while taking the time to soak up the kingdom principles that He is releasing to you. As you read this book, receive an abundance of His double-portion blessing. May God open spiritual revelation in your life in a whole new way.

I

Life Changing

Born Again

It was a beautiful sunny day in the heartland of Indiana. I was a senior then and just three weeks away from graduating. Life was loose and I was flowing with the best of them, or so I thought. I and a couple buddies (one is now passed on) chose to skip school that day and enjoy some freshly acquired marijuana laced with something extremely potent. I had smoked marijuana countless times, but my new supplier, a man over seventy years old, was into some drug making that I had not yet discovered. He was known for selling a drug that was often cutting edge in that it was experimentally mixed with other drugs. This made the demand for this particular supply hot and not easily attainable.

We sat back in our chairs, just the three of us. No one knew exactly where we were, and our parents thought we were in school like everyone else. The events that were about to unfold on this day would forever change my life. It was when God sovereignly made an appointment to capture my attention.

We all lit up, filling the room with smoke. Not much seemed to happen at first, so we kept smoking more and more and before long our minds kicked over into "dream land." This is what I call a complete control of a drug reaction. You see, we knew that this "special" stuff had been laced. We were even told to be careful because it had not been tested yet. To this day I don't know exactly what was in that marijuana bag but it was so strong that it actually caused me to stop breathing. The other two boys were fine, but not me. I could tell something was seriously wrong. I thought for a moment, *Should I call 911 and get an ambulance here, risking all three of us going to jail? Or, do I just wait it out?* I decided to do the latter.

The drug was making me laugh and laugh while my breathing got shorter and shorter. I ran into the bathroom. While looking in the mirror, I could tell something was wrong. I could not breathe at all. I tried to cry for help more than once but I could not inhale. All the air was gone and I was fading fast. Boom! I fell down onto the dirty bathroom floor right next to the nasty toilet and the old tub. I remember looking at the tub for a split second before something amazing, yet terrifying, happened.

A bright light shown right in front of me. Out of the light came Jesus and He walked straight to me, moving toward my right side. He stood next to me, looking directly at me. Then He reached His left arm around me and I felt His hand on my shoulder. Still looking at me, He whispered something in my right ear—to this day I am not sure what it was. He then looked directly at me again and said, "It's not time yet." The Lord tapped me on the left shoulder and I looked down and saw my dead body laying in that nasty old bathroom. I was looking through a bright tunnel and saw my dead, lifeless body. At that exact moment, I went flying through the portal of light down to Earth. While watching all of this in real time, I hit my body at what seemed to be mach speed. It was super fast! When my spirit slammed into my body, the breath of life blew through my lungs like the wind blowing through a jet engine. I remember gasping for air and hearing an intense sound go through my lungs and out of my mouth.

I opened my eyes and gazed at the dirty, antique tub, just inches from my face. Drool oozed out of my mouth as well as some liquid from my nose, eyes, and ear. (Of course, this could have been sweat because there was no air conditioning on at the time.) To me, it was as if my body had actually shut down for a moment and fluids started to leak out of my face.

In total amazement, I jumped to my feet screaming, "I just saw Jesus! I just saw Jesus! I just saw Jesus!" I got up, looked at my face in the mirror, and wiped it with a towel. Opening the door, I ran down the hall shouting about how I just saw God. Right at that moment, I met both of the friends I had been partying with that afternoon. One was standing in the living room gazing off and attempting to laugh at me. The other was standing on a chair and trying to dance. He barely got off the chair without falling and then harshly criticized the idea of me seeing God. Strong conviction fell on me at that moment, but I didn't know what to do about the sudden feeling of guilt and sinfulness. You see, I did not understanding the concept of a loving God. I felt He was distant, unattached, and too holy for me to ever come near to Him. I just could not imagine a divine God wanting to interrupt my life for my benefit. *Why would He want anything to do with me?*

As the conviction grew heavy upon me, I grabbed the phone. I attempted to call 911 but it did not go through! I called two more times. The first time I got a busy signal and the second time I got nothing but dead silence. Is it possible to get a busy signal dialing 911? I don't think so in the natural, and I am not going to try calling to find out. (Don't you try either!) The only explanation I have for this is that the Living God had made an appointment with me that day, and that supernatural manifestations were taking place.

Why did I call 911? It was simply a misguided conviction. I figured if I was on drugs when God showed up like that in my life, then I needed to do Him a favor and turn myself in, putting my life behind bars. That made sense to me because I did not understand grace, only the law of right and wrong. This, however, was never God's intention, nor was it His plan for my future. With that said, I believe this is why the three phone calls to 911 were also encountering divine intervention.

Since my attempts to call 911 failed, I decided to go downtown and turn myself in at the police station. As I came out of the bedroom and into the hallway, I was met by one of my drug friends. I told him that I was going to go downtown and turn myself in. He panicked and attempted to calm me down. He was still under the heavy influence of narcotics, and as we fought each other in the hallway upstairs, we suddenly found ourselves tumbling head over heels down the old, steep, wooden entry steps. Ouch! At the end of the inside steps, we were met with a screen door. The impact of our bodies hit the screen, knocking it open, and we tumbled out onto the concrete walkway. My friend jumped on top of me, grabbing my hands and pushing them to the cold concrete patio. "Lay there, man. Just lay there," he said. He got up and went back inside. Somewhat shocked, I did just as he said. I laid there for a while attempting to rationalize all that had just taken place.

It was at that moment that I realized God was so real. As I lay there outside all alone, I could feel the wind blowing, hear the birds chirping in the background, and noticed a few people walking by on the sidewalks. It was about three o'clock in the afternoon and the sun was shining. This was the precise time I would have been coming home from school that day. Everything seemed so crystal clear. For the first time in months, maybe even years, I could hear, see, and feel things that I hadn't been able to for a long time. Up to that point, I was *really* using drugs and drinking alcohol, and my body seemed to feel the effects of substance abuse. On that day everything was brand new.

The next thing I noticed was that I was absolutely in my right mind. I wasn't experiencing any effects whatsoever on my body from the drugs I had taken just an hour ago. Nothing! I was totally fine.

It was that day, at around three in the afternoon and three weeks before my high school graduation, that God made a very serious appointment with my life. He summoned me by name, capturing my heart in a way that I have never forgotten. Looking back, and recalling this event that took place all the way back in 1992, I still remember the experience as though it happened just yesterday. That day changed my life forever.

One would think that an encounter like that would turn someone's life totally right-side up. It took a little more than that for me. It wasn't

Born Again

long before I got heavily involved with alcohol—more so than a normal under-age drinker. Soon I found myself in the county jail late on a Friday night due to under-age drinking. I was not drunk or anywhere near the legal limit, but because I was only eighteen years old at the time, I got busted! They placed me in a cold holding cell that had a capacity of thirty to forty inmates. However, on that night there was no one there but me and my friend. When have you ever heard of an empty holding cell on a Friday night? Another divine appointment! My friend was released instantly and I was left there all alone. While sitting there I heard a voice say in my right ear, "Andy, now don't you think it is time to follow me?" Finally, I gave my heart to God right there alone in that cold concrete cell. Shortly after this I rededicated my life publicly in a youth group meeting on a Wednesday night. I was given one year probation and assigned to alcohol treatment classes. Within that year God spiritually grounded me with a pastor and youth pastor who invested a lot of time in my life. After one year, I was off of probation and knew that I was called to college in Springfield, MO. It was there that I met my beautiful and most amazing wife, Cathy.

I am born again!

"I was thrust into your arms at my birth. You have been my God from the moment I was born" (Psalm 22:10).

An Encounter with God

"Instantly something like scales fell from Saul's eyes, and he regained his sight. Then he got up and was baptized"(Acts 9:18).

My wife and I were living in Florida right before the turn of the century. This was before we had any children (we now have two). We had been invited to a conference in Jacksonville, Florida, for a weekend-long event through a ministry that we had never been a part of before. This ministry was, and still is, on the cutting edge of the prophetic movement in the body of Christ. So, off we went. We were all touched and I personally was blown away at the level of understanding many of the leaders carried about the knowledge of walking in and listening to the Spirit. Needless to say, this one weekend would later change my life and become a major foundational structure in why I write and now own a publishing company.

We got back late that weekend on a Sunday night and a young engaged couple, who had also been at the conference, was sitting with us at our kitchen table. We were talking and just having some great fellowship together. God had showed up at the meetings that weekend and we were still high on the presence of God and having lots of fun in the meantime.

The night grew late and we were getting ready to bring the fun-filled evening to a close, as it was a Sunday night and we all had to get up the next morning bright and early for work. God had a different plan though, and the events that were about to take place became the transformation and seal of all that you are about to read in this book. This is why I am taking the time to share with you my personal salvation experience in the previous chapter, and now this life-changing impartation that took place back in 1999.

As we were getting ready to part ways for the evening, suddenly the woman turned to me and said, "Andy, I really feel that I am supposed to pray for you and my fiancé, laying hands on you before we go." I didn't think much of it at that moment so I graciously allowed her to do so. Little did I know it was a prayer that shifted my spirit and future forever. The irony of all that is about to be shared is that since that time this family and ours have both had children and have moved on into other facets of life and ministry locations. They probably don't even realize just how much of an impact they had on my family that night. It is amazing to me how God brings someone into your life for a season to accomplish something very specific, then everything changes and life moves on. That is what happened on that night long ago. It was a divine plan because everything shifted after that, forever.

The young woman leaned forward with some anointing oil in both hands and placed her right hand on her fiancé's forehead and her left hand on mine. Her touch was very soft and gentle. God's plan that night, however, was not. God is a gentleman, but on that night He decided to bring the power out, and there was nothing gentle about it. Without going into the full details of the next two and a half hours, I want to share a few of the events I experienced. As she prayed for me, my mind began to shift back and forth from the natural and into the Spirit realm quickly. My eyes started to feel and look different and my body could feel the presence of God moving through the room and all around me. No one else that night had any type of encounter that I am aware of. In fact, I don't think any of the others felt a single thing. It just happened to be that God chose to blast me that night right there in my home.

Before long I was laughing and crying while in a vortex of the Spirit. I began to see things to come and visions of insight that have now taken place on this earth. Overwhelmed with God's touch, I remember falling out of my chair—the kind with rollers on the bottom. The chair rolled back and I fell on the extremely hard, non-forgiving Italian tile that covered the kitchen floor.

While on that cold, hard floor, my body shook violently under the power of God for nearly two and a half hours. My head banged uncontrollably on the ground over and over. Of course, no one bothered to come to my aid as my head slammed the hard tile over and over again. Finally, I got out the words "pillow...please..." The pillow helped indeed. While there on the floor I saw many amazing images of both the kingdoms of heaven and darkness. I was taken up to a mountain with the glory of the Lord and before long, laid back down on the ground in the Spirit while the great multitudes all walked by in complete unison. It was breathtaking, to say the least. God showed me the scepter of satan and a scepter of the Lord. Through all this and much more, on that night God imparted into me the ability to prophesy, and He gave me the call and tools to write.

While I was there on the floor, our friends had left to go home. The next day I reported to work—still drunk in the Spirit. I was actually approached by my students and some coworkers to have someone smell my cup to confirm I was not drunk with alcohol. I was drunk, of course, but on the freshly brewed new wine of God. This drunken stupor lasted on and off throughout the day and eventually faded. What God did in my life, however, has never faded. It was one of the events in my life that has significantly shaped and directed the destination of my calling more than any other event that I can recall. I am forever changed because of that woman's simple prayer and obedience. This story goes to show that we don't know what life-changing events can unfold through us simply because we take the time to be obedient and pray for someone. It pleases God when He tells us to pray for others and we actually do it. How many lives can radically be touched, delivered, empowered, and healed each week if Christians would be completely obedient to God's voice?

Let me briefly share the significance of this night. Just a few years before this encounter, I was placed in remedial English during my freshman year of college because my grammar and punctuation, along with my reading ability, was so horrid. Now to date, I write internationally and God has graciously allowed me to own a successful publishing company. This is what God can do in a person's life with one impartation from the hand of God.

It is through these lenses that I am writing this book. I can't possibly tell you all the precious truths the Lord placed into my heart on that Sunday night long ago. In time I will release more and more as He brings understanding to me. I personally believe that these types of encounters are happening at increased levels all over the world. I don't think God has any plans to hold back His Spirit for those who are thirsty and want to drink. It is time for us to open the doors of our hearts and let Him do a new work.

Igniting a Flame

"Praise the Lord, who is my Rock, He trains my hands for war, and gives my fingers skill for battle"(Psalm 144:1).

It was back in the summer of 2008, and my family was still traveling all over parts of the United States, primarily up and down the East Coast, and as far West as Arkansas. On one particular occasion, we were invited to a church in Cyclone, PA. What? Yes, you heard it right. According to some of the locals, this town was not near any large body of water and an actual cyclone caused major destruction in that region several years ago. Since they did not know what to name the town, they decided to name it Cyclone after the one great phenomenon that took place over that little area. With a name like Cyclone, one could only imagine what to expect when coming in to minister for the weekend. I must say that I have been to that little church more than once, and one weekend in particular changed my life for the better.

I was asked to bring my family up for a mini-conference with a man I had heard about before but had never met. In fact, I had read most of his writings some years back through a popular prophetic network. That man was Bill Yount. My family was excited to meet him.

We arrived in Cyclone and set up our 33-foot trailer in a nearby campground (we traveled with our two small children). The other guest speaker stayed in a different location. We ended up meeting before we ministered that weekend and instantly hit it off. While ministering throughout the weekend, Bill spoke on things that I was literally getting ready to speak on next. According to him, I spoke and hit on some things that he was getting ready to speak about as well. This seemed to go on throughout the entire weekend. Toward the end of the meetings, we gave Bill a CD of my wife's music and he gave me his book, *I heard Heaven Proclaim.* He signed it and then spoke over me that God was releasing a golden pen over my life to write to the nations. He took some time to explain what he meant, even telling me to read about it further in his book, which I later did. He then prayed over my hands to prophetically write and while he was praying, I felt the power of God move down through my hands, particularly my right hand. Since that day, the writings God gives me have circulated the world.

Beside the Lord, I can honestly attribute my accomplishments in writing mostly to Bill and his family. This man has been there with me along the way and he is a true man of God. I consider him a friend, mentor, and, in a few ways, a spiritual father. Since that time in 2008, his experience and wisdom has guided me through many seasons in my life. God knit my family's hearts together with Bill's, and it was definitely a divine connection.

Bill helped open the door for me to write for some very popular prophetic venues. He has cowritten some articles with me, two of which are included in this book: "Unlock the Gates" and "Hidden Oil." Bill's input in these writings is revelatory and inspiring, and I know you will enjoy his heart and transparency if you ever get a chance to meet him.

II
Time to Lead

The Unknown Prophets

*"Then Elijah said to Ahab, 'Go get something to eat and drink, for
I hear a mighty rainstorm coming!'"(1 Kings 18:41).*

While coming up out of sleep one morning, I saw a very vivid vision, which may have actually been a dream at first. During the vision I noted that powerful prophets and ministries started to fill the earth, heralding new words from God through the once-quiet lands all over the world. Some of the prophets who passed through these areas had no name or fame, yet they spoke with great authority and years later people still remembered their words.

All of these unknown prophets and the events that began to unfold over the land were appointed by God. Each one would often "hear the sound" of the Lord's new work before it had begun. This was just like Elijah who heard the sound of rain before a single drop even fell to the ground. These heralds were called for one reason as they passed through the land: they told the people in the area that a new kind of oil and fire were about to be released.

There were many acts of grace on these Christians so that even the unsaved loved to hear what they had to say. The powers these individuals carried were *love* and *favor*, and these two keys were used as weapons to change even the hardest of hearts in the territory they were assigned to.

A great season of salvation moved into the lands and many became born again. It was as if the fish jumped into the believer's very own boat. This was fishing made easy! It was an unprecedented time for souls to be saved.

Fire on the Elders

"The godly people in the land are my true heroes! I take pleasure in them!" (Psalm 16:3).

The elderly all over the world in this hour received an abundance of God's authority and power. With this in mind, many of the elderly began to push past the enemy's schemes and tricks and right into the forefront of what God was releasing on the earth. The enemy lost ground in this coming season because the elderly stepped forward. It was the unknown prophets that helped the elderly take new steps of faith.

Once the elderly in the body of Christ moved ahead, the entire kingdom advanced. The efforts of these elders brought a renewed flame to the once devastated lands. During this time, strength increased in the elderly and this created a new hope for others who followed along behind them.

Many elderly Christians think that because they are older, their time is ending and they are not useful anymore. Those in the world's society may even attempt to say that their lives are over; that they are done. Too many times the elders of our land are pushed aside, and to some they are not even valued as an asset toward life anymore.

God says in this season that He will honor the works and efforts of the elderly in the land. The Lord is saying to the elders in this time, "You are just beginning, and now I will use you more than I have used you in the past. It is through the power of your prayers that I will turn devastation into restoration. I am sending you my unknown prophets."

The sweat and tears that have fallen from the faces of the elderly will turn into flames of fire and times of joy. Those who sowed in tears will leap with a renewed joy. Through the prayers of the elderly in this hour, hidden portals into the heavenly realms will now be revealed. Many saints have cried out to God saying, "I want to see Your outpourings before I die, Lord. I want to see this promised fire before I take my last breath."

The Lord says, "In this moment, the new fire blowing over the earth will begin for your eyes to see. I will honor your hard-earned efforts." Then the Lord said to the elderly of the lands, "I am God, who keeps His promises. That which I say will come to pass."

Watch how God teams up the unknown prophets with the elders of the land. This will become as powerful as a spark to gasoline. The relationship will become an unstoppable force against the enemy. Young prophets need elders just as much as elders need prophets.

Mantles in the Sky

"'The time will come,' says the Lord, 'when the grain and grapes will grow faster than they can be harvested. Then the terraced vineyards on the hills of Israel will drip with sweet wine! I will bring my exiled people of Israel back from distant lands, and they will rebuild their ruined cities and live in them again. They will plant vineyards and gardens; they will eat their crops and drink their wine'" (Amos 9:13-14).

Recently, as I was falling asleep one night, I saw detailed images of mantles falling from heaven on the earth. These mantles resembled millions of robes, and many of the finely-crafted pieces had a specific name written on them. It definitely was a fascinating scene to go to bed to! Although there is much to conclude about this sight, we must ask, "What is God trying to say here?" If we are not diligent when the Lord gives us something, it can easily be treated with contempt. We quickly read into only one part that "stuck out" of what God revealed, and miss the other hundred pieces of insight that He was also trying to show us. This easily happens by speaking, acting, and moving too fast on something God gave us, when He really wanted us to "chew on it" for a long time before releasing the information. Luke 2:19 says, "but Mary kept all these things in her heart and thought about them often." She did this because she knew it was not time for the world to know. This is the same way we need to approach the things God gives us—meditate on the visions and dreams to discover more than what we first see or perceive.

The mantles I saw represented the traits, gifting, and deity of Christ resting on the earth in greater strength. There were many different names on these robes. Some were names of God and others were names of people—both alive today and passed on. As these glorious robes touched different parts of the world, it was noticeable that some of them carried the same distinct traits as others did. And though various mantles remained empty for a long time, others were quickly filled, as if the person was at the right place at the right time. A divine collision between the person and mantle took place here in this fascinating event.

These robes that were falling into the new era had noticeably strong regional and assigned authorities upon them. This gave authenticity to the commissioning of the person who received them. Without a doubt, this was a personal and divine impartation from the hand of God. The Lord backed these mantles with a generational breakthrough power that made callings complete in due time. Easily seen, these robes affected many generations to come.

While watching this spectacular event unfold from the sky, God gave this insight:

> *"Elijah went over to him and threw his cloak across his shoulders"*
> *(1 Kings 19:19).*

> *"Elisha picked up Elijah's cloak, which had fallen when he was taken up. Then Elisha returned to the bank of the Jordan River" (2 Kings 2:13).*

Parallel these two Scriptures together with me for just a moment and some of you will discover where you are and what is about to happen. In 1 Kings, the initial commissioning took place from Elijah to Elisha. This is where most people are—they have begun, but have not been fully activated by the new double portion, found in 2 Kings. What happened then was that the chariots picked up Elijah and dropped Elijah's mantle to Elisha. POW! A spiritual explosion took place, producing the actual manifestation of the glorious new double portion over Elisha's life. Thus, Elijah's last miracle became Elisha's first. The new manifestation of the double portion is now on Elisha in greater power than it actually was on Elijah. God already gave the initial dimensions of many of your callings and commissions ("1 Kings" encounter). Now it's time for the "2 Kings" encounter, which is both mantles colliding in the Spirit at once! Some of you are in between the 1 Kings and the 2 Kings realm.

These falling robes represent the 2 Kings "double portion." In a double-portion scenario there are two mantles bearing large amounts of fruit at the exact same time. This creates rapid growth and accelerated maturation of the body of Christ. Elijah's mantle came upon Elisha as the chariots of fire went up. Did Elijah's mantle stop functioning at that time? NO! It increased and was released in greater power and capacity than when it was resting on Elijah. Now Elijah's and Elisha's mantle are both fully functioning in power. What was once hard to plow can now be easily sown and reaped at the same time. This is a double portion anointing.

The anointing (mantle) is from God, but imparted to many different people. This is the key ingredient! God will drop mantles in abundance on all flesh. That means you! Elijah carried a mantle similar to John the Baptist. They both came as forerunners to Jesus Christ. They boldly fought against religion. Elisha's mantle, however, also looks similar to the mantle of Jesus. They were both twice as affective as their predecessors. Elisha and Jesus stood before the rich all the way down to the lowly and poor.

The mantles I saw in the vision will be more intensified than in times past. What appeared to be unfinished with some of the past mantle carriers will become complete in the years ahead. Just like Elisha functioned with his and Elijah's covering, so will it be with these carriers. In all reality, these mantles are really from the Lord Himself. These are just trickles of what is coming. As these robes land on their rightful owners, they will spark many creative and unusual encounters.

Note that many mantles fell together and at once. Expect the unexpected when you gather together. Unity is your weapon in this season. This is imperative in the coming years. Remember, it is only the beginning stages of what is later to come. Why did Elisha function so well in the prophetic, and with so much force? It was because he was operating in two mantles at once. Unity is a must!

Mantles of Revolution

"Instead, we will speak the truth in love, growing in every way more and more like Christ, who is the head of his body, the church" (Ephesians 4:15).

In the vision of the mantles falling from the sky, one particular mantle created a standard against heresy. When these specific mantles came into contact with their owners, those people became bold and persuasive in speech like the Apostle Paul. The Lord released a heavy presence upon these individuals, causing people to flock to them and hear what they had to say. They spoke freedom and grace only by the cross. The more they spoke, the stronger the anointing became. Truth surrounded their hearts and minds. Discernment protected every word from their mouth. Many yokes of religion were broken.

This mantle that came to rest on the land reminded me of Martin Luther:

Martin Luther lived from 1483–1546. He founded Protestantism, one of the major movements within Christianity out of the Catholic Church. He was a German monk, theologian, university professor, priest, and church reformer whose ideas started the Protestant Reformation and changed the course of Western civilization. Luther taught that salvation is a free gift of God and received only through true faith in Jesus as redeemer from sin, not from work or good deeds. His theology challenged the authority of the pope of the Roman Catholic Church by teaching that the Bible is the only source of Christian doctrine and all baptized Christians are priests before God (priesthood of all believers). His reformation began by the publication of his 95 Theses in 1517 against the claims of indulgent preachers that God's punishment for sins could be avoided by buying them. Luther's refusal to retract his writings at the demand of the pope in 1520, and the Holy Roman Emperor Charles V at the Diet of Worms meeting in 1521, resulted in his excommunication by Pope Leo X and condemnation as an outlaw by the emperor. He wrote in the language of the people, (German instead of Latin), and made it more accessible, causing a tremendous impact on the church and German culture. It fostered the development of a standard version of the German language, added several principles to the art of translation, and influenced the translation of the King James Bible.[1]

In order to be a reformer, one must make a whole-hearted choice to live and die for what they believe in. What is it that motivates you? Is there a dream or passion within your heart that is so personal and life changing to you that you are willing to do anything to see it come to pass? The answer to those two questions will help you understand what exactly you are a reformer of. To be a reformer, you must know what you are attempting to change and reform. I believe God has called you to change the earth and make a mark on society. What are you waiting for? Well, let me answer that question for you. You are probably waiting for the right amount of insurance coverage or the money for this project to fall from a tree. My friend, if this is the case, you may be waiting for a long time. I believe a reformer is one who has every reason to make an excuse, but chooses to use none. A reformer cares so much about their call to reform a particular situation that they don't care what it costs or if they will outlive their opponents. Reformers just simply go and get the job done at all cost. This is the mantle I see falling through the heavens and touching down on Earth. The revolution carriers rising up will be like none ever seen. The Church is finally being born again.

---

1. Wikipedia contributors, "Martin Luther," Wikipedia, The Free Encyclopedia, http://en.wikipedia.org/w/index.php?title=Martin_Luther&oldid=439895744 (accessed July 21, 2011).

The Pioneer and Inventive Mantle

*"This is what Cyrus king of Persia says: "The Lord, the God of
Heaven, has given me all the kingdoms of the earth and He has
appointed me to build a temple for Him at Jerusalem in Judah"
(2 Chronicles 36:23).*

This mantle is like the creative sojourners of those on the Mayflower. They were not afraid to take risks when the hand of God was upon them. These people will carry the creative and inventive ideas that are not confined to past inventions. The inventors will get their thoughts directly from the Father. They are the Benjamin Franklins of our day—the ones who see beyond the lightning in the sky and envision an entire city filled with lights. These mantles of design will create a completely new era of thinking. Many lives will be forever changed by some of the inventions coming on the earth from these Christians. I believe the funding from just one of these inventions will create enough money to financially free ministries for their entire duration of service.

Take a look at Mr. Marpeck:

*Mr. Marpeck was born in 1495, in Rattenberg, Austria. In 1527 he was
ordered by the government to persecute Anabaptists, whom he himself
was. He worked his way into business and political realms influencing
both, and at the same time figured out how to educate and mentor the
Anabaptist. In 1528, his belongings and property were seized; he then*

took on a different life to flee from further persecution. He moved to Strasbourg and was hired to manage the city's timber operations, which also included the entire section of the timber transport by river. It was here he came up with an idea to revolutionize the weaving industry by establishing a bleaching operation for the entire community.

Being that the industries were all built, at the time, along the waterways, those further distances from the water were poorer due to lack of trade and production. Marpeck came up with the idea of storing water higher up to produce pressure in the water so that the areas away from the river could have what we now call "piped and pressurized water." This opened up an entire new door for industry in regions that otherwise would have never had anything but dry dirt. His creative and intuitive thoughts propelled him in 1550 to Public Works Director of the entire region. In spite of those still wanting to persecute him, his inventions put him in greater demand than for the grave. During this entire time, he set right under the noses of people that wanted him dead because he consistently wrote to the growing movement of the Anabaptist, which at the time was illegal. God gave him such favor and authority in creativity that many overlooked that he was a fugitive.[2]

This goes to show how powerful a creative mantle really is. It is one that can prolong your life and affect many people around you. Complete communities were touched by just one mantle. As this mantle stood hovering over the earth, it was apparent that those who would soon carry this precious commodity were folks who did not have selfish motives. They were not the hoarders of their time nor the greedy. Like a seed planted in the ground, funds (currency) began to flow through these mantles. The more the carriers released to others, the more God watered their seed. They were believers who loved to give more than they received.

For way too long in our local churches we have become accustomed to "killing" out any form of creativity that does not mix or blend with our current church and social status. Take the famous porn owners for starters. They were once kids and probably graced some good ole' church

2. Wally Kroeker, "He Would Have Made a Great MEDA Member," The Marketplace (March/April 2009): 16-17.

services just like you and I. Their gifts were obviously different as they were called to create the beauty of art through human expressions. When the anointing would hit them, they would draw beautiful people, not like when the anointing hit Bertha and she would sing, or when the anointing hit Harry and he would dance. What happens when the anointing hits you? Well, when it hits me, I preach, prophesy, write, and see an abundance of creative gifts touching lives.

Not so with the future porn guru as a child. He was passionate about pure body expression and the church, at the time, did not see it and therefore, they refused to recognize that gift within him. Why? It was different! It did not match the board's agenda for remodeling the basement. It did not fit with the pulpit committee's opinions on what types of messages should or should not be developed within the church. Therefore, Little Future Porn Star, like so many other people in the church, got kicked out of the pew and into the streets. And you know what happened then? He met satan who came along and said, "Hey, little boy, that church stinks, doesn't it? Church life is bad for you and you just don't fit in. So, little boy, come with me and I will show you a whole new world of body parts that will satisfy all your cravings for the creative realm of the human anatomy like you have never imagined it before." Off they went, the little porn star and satan. They took off together and have since destroyed millions of lives through the hook of pornography, when all along this young boy could have been working for Jesus—painting and creating some of the greatest and most pure forms of illustrative human art on earth. Church needs to change! It must happen and it will. Open your doors to the realm of the creative gifts of God and you will discover immeasurable amounts of a free flowing creativity unlike anything you can imagine.

Undiscovered Mantles

"I have been following the plan spoken of in the Scriptures, where it says, 'Those who have never been told about him will see, and those who have never heard of him will understand'" (Romans 15:21).

While watching mantles all over touch people's lives, I understood what some of the mantles represented. Unlike many of the mantles already, there was a particular mantle that was revealed at a much later time than the rest. This robe was so different from the others. It was not shaped like the other coverings and had no name either. It had many rare and distinct colors unlike any I have ever seen. It was exquisitely brilliant. At some instances, you could see a reflection upon the mantle. At other times, one could see right through it, but you knew it was still there. It was as if the material was reflective, transparent, and mixed with undiscovered colors all at the same moment. Sensational, for lack of a better word!

This is the Lord's creative, unseen, and undiscovered dimensions that have not touched man's comprehension yet. Yes, we know a lot about Jesus. Many can talk about Him day and night, but there is still much more to be discovered. Imagine looking into space or going into the depths of the oceans for the first time. Wouldn't it feel like a whole new world? This is how I feel about this spectacular mantle. Obviously, this splendid robe was on the earth when Jesus came because He is truth and in Him is completion. This extraordinary mantle solely represents the many undiscovered and unseen aspects of Jesus Christ.

"Jesus also did many other things. If they were all written down, I suppose the whole world could not contain the books that would be written" (John 21:25).

There were more of this mantle than any other one. This robe fell last, yet brewed on the earth longer than them all. This is new. It is being unveiled like a child in the womb. You know it is there. You feel it. Briefly, you have touched it. Most of all you know it is real. But we have not fully laid hold of it like we will begin to in the coming years. These are the unseen and undiscovered dimensions of God. The Lord's realm of new enlightenment and gleaming glory has finally begun.

There are a lot of gifts out there waiting to be discovered. For instance, when I was a young child, I never thought of writing a book, nor did I realize that I would one day own an internationally distributed publishing company. The thought of both are still breathtaking in some ways. God had plans and both were part of them for my life. Through the years and looking back, I see how God has adjusted each phase of my life to properly lead me into what I am currently doing. This is how an undiscovered mantle works. It often is one that you walk into and did not even realize that it was what God had called for you all along. Ever notice that some of the greatest singers out there cannot often times even read a note? My wife is like that. She cannot read music notes very well, but you can find her music on some radio stations here and there. How is that? It is the God-given ability of the undiscovered mantle. When she was playing and creating music long into the night, she did not realize that one day her music would be on the radio. Looking back, God gave her more responsibility and many undiscovered mantles to prepare her for her destiny.

You don't have to understand the entire map of life, you just have to know who created the trail for you. Stop trying to figure it all out and learn to work hard in what God has asked you to oversee today. Tomorrow, you just might walk right into an undiscovered mantle that is your very own.

End Time Generals

"So he started out, and he (Phillip) met the treasurer of Ethiopia, a eunuch of great authority" (Acts 8:27).

During worship, I saw what appeared to be a devastated land with a disjointed army. It appeared that the soldiers had been under intense battles for an extended season. As I looked closer, it was not the "battering" that was the issue; the problem was the soldiers were all present but not in unity. There were many people on the same side, but they were all in different clusters, facing many directions and lacking the ability to understand who the real leaders were in each group.

As I looked out across the battlefield, I was rather confused as to what they were doing. There were many voices and much movement, but little progress. Then right before my eyes, people (actually, they were kingdom generals and they didn't even know it) from each cluster grabbed swords and mustered the troops. Each little cell became one again, like a mighty brigade. In the natural, I thought each huddle of fighting warriors was about to go out to their own locations and take territory, but to my surprise, the exact opposite happened. Each kingdom general, with swords held high, gathered their small clusters, then proceeded to come together as one body and began to advance as one massive army.

This force was unstoppable from every direction. Their voices were filled with powerful faith as if they were breathing fire out of their mouths. These once-battered soldiers very quickly became spiritual, flaming infernos against the enemy. The Lord's presence on these "kingdom soldiers" was burning brighter than usual. Each fire fed off of another's fire, like hot coals under dry, burning wood. The spiritual heat from this advancing army was like the sun. This was intense. It is the image of the great kingdom army coming on the entire earth as one body and one voice. Every believer globally united!

This is the great day of unity coming all over the world for the body of Christ. Regardless of the denomination, fellowship, or Christian-based belief system you are involved in, you remain a part of an ever increasing power that has an endless supply from heaven. Now is the time to encourage unity and bring it into your region. We don't need more churches until we can learn to live in unity with the ones we already have.

Generals All Over the World

"Meanwhile, Philip found himself farther north at the town of Azotus. He preached the Good News there and in every town along the way until he came to Caesarea" (Acts 8:40).

I heard the Lord say, "You will know and recognize My leaders, but I will personally commission them. They will know and hear My voice, truly leading My people, steering them where I need them to go as one. These generals (kingdom leaders) will all have a common root system that I have placed within them, and that is the concept My children must understand regarding unity and power. They are not government army leaders from a worldly standpoint (though some will be trained by the government military), these new generals will be trained in kingdom strategy by divine authority, which far outweighs natural military tactics.

"My kingdom will become so advanced so suddenly that My children will start training government leaders and military in how new strategies can be implemented to save time, money, and lives. A new level of leadership is coming on the scene in My kingdom. You will see them start to take their positions and seats over the regions that I have called them to. Many have already made reference to the coming years as the apostolic working, however, right now is the season for My 'general positioning.' Prepare yourselves as one body to receive My 'kingdom generals.' They have been forged and trained through their own desert experiences, and now they are ready for battle and advancement.

"In the past seasons, many communities have advanced like locusts, either without leadership, or with many leaders each having their own strategies. This is no longer allowed for the preparation of the global awakening that is coming on the earth. In a body structure, when the toe is in pain, the brain feels it, and the leg compensates to carry the load of the injured toe.

"Now you must learn to connect in the exact places you belong. Not everyone can be a head or foot, but everyone must be joined to the body at the right place to advance further. The kneecap is not designed to be connected to a rib. It is designed to be placed on the leg. Find the place where you belong. Learn to walk together in your region as one advancing force under My direct orders."

Equipping Generations

"We will build a tower of redemption to protect her. Since she is vulnerable we will enclose her with a wall of cedar boards" (Song of Songs 8:9-10, TPT).

Through a personal encounter, the Lord showed me how the flames in some regions, that once had been heavily damaged, eventually burned so hot that they started sparking into distant lands in other parts of the earth. Within a short time, there were massive spiritual infernos burning in every country of the world.

Every part of the world was touched by a new level of release found in the increase of equipping those that were coming into future leadership upon the earth. The transition from one generation to the next was marvelous. This time the power continued on from one generation to the next because the wisdom and integrity of the elders kept the flames burning.

There were few who were spiritually fatherless in this coming equipping era. True authority was upon the younger leaders because they understood exactly who they were in Christ, and they were totally free. That freedom was rooted in the fact that the elderly stood their ground and watched over the upcoming, future generations of the earth.

These spiritually mature "fireballs" that were released out upon the earth were the equippers to prepare for the coming harvest. They are the flames of the kingdom that are called to create a stable platform for others to safely learn to walk on. It is their patient and compassionate efforts that will one day allow a whole body of believers to fly like eagles on their own.

Through the determination and leadership of these saints, the era of a whole new way of equipping will soon be ignited in the earth, allowing those that walk behind their leaders to one day walk safely on their own. These are the keepers of the coming flames. Are you ready to be set on fire?

All the Numbers on the Clock Turned to Twelve

"For God says, 'At just the right time, I heard you. On the day of salvation, I helped you.' Indeed, the 'right time' is now. Today is the day of salvation" (2 Corinthians 6:2).

In a recent dream and while coming up out of my sleep, I saw an analog clock and both hands hit the twelfth number at the top. In that precise moment, all the other numbers (1-11) fell off the clock and were all replaced by the number twelve. I heard in the Spirit, *The clock strikes midnight and this is a new dawn.* I immediately thought, *This is the end of the night and the beginning of the breaking of the dawn. This is the coming age of the 'multiple twelves.'*

Some of you reading this have been walking in the night hours, the most painful hours of your life. You have wondered more than once about how you were possibly going to make it to the next minute. In some cases, those reading this have even thought about ending it all. It is time to prepare to leave your moments of pain and walk out in full daylight. Your Redeemer comes quickly! He is the God of compassion and mercy. He has been watching over you all this time and is pleased to act on your behalf. Do not give up. Press on!

What do the twelve numbers represent? The twelve numbers represent the Lord overwriting the weaker numbers within a system or structure. Twelve, as you know, is the highest level on the clock. This is an example of what happens when God's grace overwrites our weak areas in life. When a larger number overtakes a weaker one, the highest prevails. This, my friend is a sure sign of the Lord's covering in all areas of your life. The highest is here!

Not only did the clock strike twelve midnight, but the moment this happened twelves appeared all over the clock and replaced all the other numbers. A whole clock of twelves! In other words, a whole "flock" of twelves are about to take over. This vivid imagery is a reminder of the real and genuine apostolic movement that is promised by God to come on display at the end of the procession and before the Lord's day. This is a sign that the Lord is sewing into place the apostolic garment that is full of power and kingdom authority. Many have embraced apostolic movements within our church systems that have worked great up to this point, but I believe we have not seen the real amplification and power of a manifested apostolic movement on this earth yet. God is not getting done with the apostolic work of the church; He is just starting! God is a God of "new numbers." He is perfect in multiplication and timing.

"Over My people, I will release new numbers that will overwrite the numbers that were lacking. I AM is what I had them say in the days of Moses. I AM is what you will echo all over your land. I AM the great God of mercy and power, able to sustain when no food is present. I AM will bring rain in the deserts and snow in the hot lands. I will reveal new water in dry lands. I will raise up new government authorities both within countries and within the Christian communities."

Right after this direct word from the Lord, I saw praise reports, testimonies, and spontaneous miracles popping up all over the earth like popcorn in a hot kettle. Sudden disasters turned into divine opportunities for supernatural miracles. Christians were prepared and ready. They led the front lines of disaster relief, allowing God to work through them to produce miracle after miracle. The bad land was restored through Christians, not a government program.

At the closing of this dream with the clock, I saw an old prophet that stood on a rock overlooking the mountain. He turned to the new (younger) prophet that was standing on a lower rock beside the older prophet and then passed the baton to him. The baton is soon to be passed from one generation to the next. "Well done, good and faithful servant!" Many current fathers of the faith are getting ready to slow down and prepare for their final stages of life on this earth. It is now time for a new generation of leaders to pick up where the fathers of the faith will one day leave off.

III

Going Forth

Spiritual Cross-Pollination

"...as they (Philip and the Ethiopian) rode along (together)..."
(Acts 8:36).

In the Spirit, I saw missionaries packing their bags again. Due to lack of funds, some came off the field but are about to go back. Many have been called and are waiting, but let it be said to you: Pack your bags and prepare by faith! Churches opened their pulpits once again, allowing the real fullness of God to manifest freely. During this time, I heard the Spirit say, "Open your pulpits, open your doors, open your gates and go into your cities. *Advance* is the word for your community."

After these words, I noticed that bees were flying everywhere, not attacking the kingdom, but cross-pollinating the kingdom. There was so much cross-pollination taking place that it was too numerous to count. The bees were coming from every direction, all over the earth. This caused the enemy to lose ground in the attempt to stop this global kingdom shift.

This era the body of Christ is entering into over the next several years will involve the strongest and most active cross-pollination of the kingdom of heaven on earth than any time over the past several decades. Expect new territory, new acquaintances, divine appointments, and many new relationships. While watching the bees, the Lord then said, "When I do a new work in a person's life with a new season, it will always require shedding the old wineskins and forging into the new wineskins. When this begins to happen, know for sure new relationships and people will play a major part of My working." Many of you reading this are about to meet some people that will be responsible for connecting you to your destiny.

Come Out of the Storm Shelter

"Upon arriving in Antioch, they called the church together and
reported everything God had done through them and how he had
opened the door of faith to the Gentiles, too" (Acts 14:27).

In a dream, there were storm shelter doors opening all over the world. Underground bunkers started opening on every major continent. Christians came up out of these bunkers with a mighty force. Many had battened down the hatches, which had been needed for this past season, in order to protect their lives. During this next season, God will open the hatches and let His children arise.

In any battle, the side that eventually outwits, out maneuvers, and out works their opponent will normally win. What happens when both sides bunker down, like in the days of trench warfare, where one trench is dug on one side and then another is dug on the other? It turns into a brutal game that just goes back and forth until someone decides to advance through other means and never retreat again. As Christians, there is a time to retreat and bow out gracefully in a battle. There is also a time to hide under the shelter of God and just wait out the storm. There is also a time, and I believe it is now for many, to come up out of the shelter and trenches and destroy the enemy's plans once and for all. It is time to grab the sword and attack. This day we must fight!

The Lord is saying, "For the past few years many in My kingdom have been scared and disillusioned with all the changes and shaking that has come upon the earth. Fear is the enemy's plan to slow your pace and get you out of alignment from My steps. For some of you this has worked, but I say to you now, open the hatches and move out with the shield of faith. It is time to go back on the fields of battle to conquer, not to retreat. When My children gather, they will advance. In natural wars currently taking place in this season, I will show exploits and create heroes that will raise the bar and define a whole new level of valor."

Unlock the Gates

"Great is his faithfulness; his mercies begin afresh each morning"
(Lamentations 3:23).

In a dream on July 4, 2009 at 2:48 AM, a door closed directly behind me and then another door (more like a gate) opened, and I walked through it. Right before waking up, the Lord spoke these words: "This is an era closing and a new one beginning." We are starting a totally new era on this earth. Not a new season, but a completely new epoch. It is as impacting as going from the old steam engines to bullet trains, or moving from horse and buggy to electric hybrid cars. The former systems are fading quickly. It is time to let the old wineskins officially die. Close the doors of the past and open the gates of the future.

Is your system changing fast? This year, practically every imaginable adjustment that can come is happening. For example, our computer finally gave up, and as a result, God gave us two for the price of one. The insurance that we used to have has now been exchanged for a completely new program. Just a year ago I would have said "absolutely no" to this type of medical coverage. When we stepped out on the road full time (June 30, 2006), we got rid of a dog, but just this year God gave us back an incredible one, perfectly fit for travel. Recently, God paid some of our bills off in a day's time. I could go on and on, both in the natural and spiritual. The fact is that things are happening in new realms.

THINGS *to* COME

The earth is quickly changing and taking on a completely new form. Japan's earthquake, along with many recent disasters, have actually altered time and global geographical maps. Indeed we are facing a whole new pattern on earth. With this said, the way we conduct life in general will change dramatically. What happens in other countries will immediately affect the United States. Regardless of if we like it or not, every organization that plans on surviving the next century will need to learn how to adapt to the global economy and adjust rapidly. This is not going to be an easy task. Things we work on for a season and then leave alone are suddenly brought back onto the scene and adjusted again. It often reminds me of building a massive wall one brick at a time. This is what Nehemiah did and he did it with superb skill and craftsmanship.

Whatever you are dealing with now must be consistently monitored and adjusted on a regular basis or it will not survive the coming economic disasters and shifts. One key element to all this is learning to have multiple streams of income. The days of growing up in your hometown, getting a great paying job with benefits, and retiring right there on the same block you grew up on is completely over. Do we like this? Absolutely not! But, we must learn to deal with it now and adjust. In my generation, leaving town for better education and jobs are just common practice. Sooner than later, the next generation will be leaving the country for better education and careers. This is going to happen and we must prepare the body of Christ for it as best we can. If you have younger children, get them ready for living in other countries now while there is still time.

For example, there was a temporal change that stunned us for a long time. Because of being on staff and pastoring for nine years, I was accustomed to being in a suit and tie on Sundays. When we stepped out on the road several years ago, Cathy and I felt the Lord tell us to dress nice, but not in dresses and suits anymore. A while back, we went to a church who would not let Cathy minister in prophetic worship because she did not have a dress on. Now I know what you probably want to say, "That religious group of people!" This is what I thought at first.

Then God showed me a different side. As I talked this over with a friend of mine, the Spirit of the Lord came upon him saying, "Andy, you are going into a new season and territory where you must be ready to humble yourselves and put on a tie, with Cathy in a dress, if it is required of you to minister there. Don't miss a God opportunity because of the way you want to look. You must be meek and willing to meet the people you minister to by going there as a servant of the Lord, not for any other reason." Then he said, "What if God has truly asked those churches to dress nice on a Sunday?"

Since that time, we have decided to be more in season, and therefore the blessings and anointing have increased. No wonder the Apostle Paul said in 1 Corinthians 10:31-33, "So whether you eat or drink, or whatever you do, do it all for the glory of God. Don't give offense to Jews or Gentiles or the church of God. I, too, try to please everyone in everything I do, I don't just do what is best for me; I do what is best for others so that many may be saved."

Bill Yount also had a similar experience that he shared with me. He said, "I remember when I first got saved and had longer hair over my ears. I went to a certain church with an evangelist, and he had asked me to come along to sing a song. Before the service began the pastor took me into a side room and explained that I could not sing in this church because my hair was over my ears. After the service that night I went home thinking, 'God looks at the heart and not our hair, and their religious spirit caused them to miss hearing a great anointed song.'

"Going to bed that night the Lord began talking to me. 'Son, which is more important to you for eternity—the length of your hair or ministering the Gospel? Are you going to let the length of your hair stop you from ministering the Gospel?' I realized that wanting to keep my hair long was just as religious as they wanting it short. Since I got my hair cut, there hasn't been a church that has a problem with the length of my hair.

"Also, concerning appearance, I used to be bound by wearing a tie all of the time in church since I was raised that way. Then I thought that real freedom was not having to wear a tie. I later learned that I am only free indeed when I can wear one or go without one, and it doesn't bother me either way! In regards to the length of hair, I should be free enough to grow it long again if it is to help relate to people that God has me minister to as well.

"What I'm saying is this: Do not miss what God is about to do in your life because it cramps your style. This next era will be distinct with many implausible paths and open gates. If we aren't careful, we will walk as a persistent old wineskin that is undying to change, instead of moving in true servant humility.

"We must allow our agendas to expire and learn to live for the Lord's plans. This requires deep humility and mature faith. The Lord is saying now, 'Be prepared to do big things. Be enthusiastic to do the small and temporal in order to bring something great in another's life.' God has to break and cleanse us with the water of humility in order to display the shining spiritual diamonds that are hidden deep within."

Take a Close Look at the Israelites

" 'Scout out the land on the other side of the Jordan River,
especially around Jericho.' So the two men set out and came to the
house of a prostitute named Rahab and stayed there that night"
(Joshua 2:1).

God used such an abnormal condition to later bring transformation. God's methods can be challenging to our patterns. God was setting up something totally new. He will do this in many lives. In spite of the fact she was a sinner, Rahab's household was spared. Then God blessed her womb to be part of the greatest genealogy of all time: Jesus Christ. In this new era, God will call the prostitutes of our nation back to Him. Like Rahab, their wombs will be blessed and they will lead large regions for Christ.

"Salmon was the father of Boaz (whose mother was Rahab).
Boaz was the father of Obed (whose mother was Ruth). Obed

was the father of Jesse. Jesse was the father of King David"
(Matthew 1:5-6).

What if the Israelites would have said, "No! This can't be God." They might have missed it! We must get ready to work with people that have rough edges. In fact, the person who you don't like just might be the fertilizer that God has sent your way to help you grow into His likeness! Be alert, they are coming to do you good!

Ask Joseph how he made it to the palace and, at some point, his testimony will be filled with the wickedness of his brothers. He will tell you about the thirteen long years he spent in prison and even encountered Potiphar's wicked wife. He will probably not tell you much about the palace itself, but he will make sure you understand how he got there and the people God used in his life. Looking back he will tell you that his dream was so big that God chose to use his enemies to unwrap it!

God still seems to use the enemy's plans to bring out the best in us! You and I may have old wineskins hanging on that must go in order to prepare for the lost to enter the kingdom. This is an era that is changing on the entire earth. God's ways may not come about exactly how we planned, nor will it look precisely how we thought. We need to be flexible to handle the new strategies of the Holy Spirit. God's plans may look very unusual!

Remember that Rahab was spared. "It was by faith that Rahab the prostitute was not destroyed with the people in her city who refused to obey God. For she had given a friendly welcome to the spies" (Hebrews 11:31).

Remember too, that one door shut and another larger gate-like door opened. As this happens we must be like the men of Israel. They were pure enough to stay the night in a prostitutes den, yet they remained faithful and spotless before the Lord. (Do not attempt this in the natural, men!) This is walking in the fruit of the Spirit. Get ready for unexpected plans to unfold in your life as you become a light in a darkened world.

Fire in the Land

"So that day Moses solemnly promised me, 'The land of Canaan on which you were just walking will be your grant of land and that of your descendants forever, because you wholeheartedly followed the Lord my God'"(Joshua 14:9).

The Lord recently released a vision to me relating to parts of the earth that had been destroyed by natural disasters. He showed how this devastation turned from a natural disaster into a Spirit-burning fire within the hearts of people and then into many parts of the world. The holy fire began to burn bright in areas that were once physically devastated.

In the Spirit, one could hear the sound of these infernos roaring like a lion as the flames shot a great height into the skies. This brought a spiritual beacon for many to know where to go and to take their next steps of faith. Before this, people were wondering what the next path would entail for their lives. Once the light of God's presence burned higher over the skies of these devastated lands, they began to walk right into their next destinations.

There were many people in these once-devastated areas, that were still holding on, waiting to encounter the promises of God's words once spoken. These prophetic words spoken over them were about to come to pass. People throughout the land were once again reminded of what God said He would do for them. These remembered promises brought excitement in the air.

While the spiritual fires began to burn bright over these lands, the promised words exploded into the hearts of the people, bringing much needed encouragement for this hour. The spiritual climate over the lands during this time also erupted like volcanoes, decreeing righteousness and grace for the people in these areas.

Translation, the Kingdom Way of Transportation

"When they came up out of the water, the Spirit of the Lord snatched Philip away. The eunuch never saw him again but went on his way rejoicing" (Acts 8:39).

The Lord is saying, "In some cases, I am going to keep some of My children right where they are in the natural, but the release of translation will manifest upon them. Some of you reading this writing will be awakened and shaken by the translated 'Philips' of our time. Translation will eventually become a normal manifestation of the kingdom of heaven on earth. I will use these supernatural events to speed up the process of global cross-pollination."

You are seeing it more and more with sci-fi Hollywood movies these days. God did it first and He will do it again and again. I have personally met people in my travels who have shared stories of how they were in one spot physically yet in another location in the Spirit. On at least one occasion, I know I have been translated before, maybe even twice. I am not going to take the time to go into details here, but I will say that one occurrence was when I was leaving to go on the road full time and for the first time back in 2006. To describe these occurrences will require another book at another time.

However, the accounts are increasing all over the world and this is very real stuff. We are in a new dispensational era where time has sped up, knowledge is increasing rapidly, and the gospel is being spoken to all over the world. The imminent return of Christ is drawing nearer with a stronger reality upon the earth of His soon return. With that in mind, God's people are being used more and more in a supernatural way. Why? God is determined to get the message of His Son, Jesus Christ, to as many people as possible.

Some reading this might think that it is not possible for one to be translated. Scientifically it may be easier than what you realize with the advancement of modern technology. The phone lines are transmitting sounds. Faxes are transmitting ink images. The internet transmits just about anything now and it doesn't even require a land line. With all that said, even cell phones can do just about anything you want them to now. We are living in a day where rapid movement is happening by the second. In order to keep up with this all the time, many will find themselves being translated on a regular basis as we get closer to the Lord's return. Don't rule out the concept of translation, besides it is in the New Testament (see Acts chapter 8).

A Moving River Will Transport Life

*"Therefore I, a prisoner for serving the Lord, beg you to lead
a life worthy of your calling, for you have been called by God"
(Ephesians 4:1).*

In a dream a while back God showed me something very profound: A young man stood with two other helpers. He was of age, clean cut, and a handsome man. He decided on his own to walk through a new door for his life. This door would lead him to a very dangerous country, and he knew it. When he stepped forward in confidence, knowing it was the will of God and possibly at the cost of his own life one day, the two other helpers stepped forward and followed. This one step changed the course of many lives for decades to come.

What is God saying in this dream? This season is not a season of indecisiveness. It is a season of divine confidence from God to man. It is a season to choose your weapons and battles wisely. Know the path that God has placed before you and stick to it. Step forward in confidence, knowing that it is God who called you. He will cause others to step in faith with you. You will not walk alone in this coming season. As you move forward in the plans that God has for you, others will see the call and follow to help. Time to move forward! A stale pond breeds toxin, but a moving river transports life. It is certainly time for the bride of

Christ to move forward again. As we step forward to gain more territory for the Lord's kingdom, the presence of God will put our lives in order and cause us to keep the ground we just obtained.

New Lands to Dwell In

"Enlarge your house; build an addition. Spread out your home, and spare no expense!" (Isaiah 54:2).

While in the Spirit one day, I looked out over many regions and cities and I saw a brewing frustration of stagnation within the hearts of many people. It has been the enemy's plans once again to stop the kingdom's advancement. When the flow of movement is ceased, it causes stagnation. The enemy wants as much territory that he can get. One way he is attempting to stop the body of Christ right now is through delaying the process of owning a home. Having a home releases legal rights, both in the natural and spiritual realms, to take claim over that county and territory. At the time of this writing the tax breaks between owning your own home and renting are extremely different. Owning your own home is obviously more beneficial at this current time. Many have said, "I have no home, I have no place to go." This has been the enemy's plan, to send some of you wandering aimlessly in the wilderness.

The Lord says, "Drive your stake in your territory. Pour out the oil on the land. Gather the people to worship and pray over your land, because I am not taking away territory in this season; I am giving it." Gather them in now to change the atmosphere over the territory of that region, and the natural laws will fall into place to favor the verdicts over your properties. To say it's time for God's people to advance is an understatement!

They Will Stand Amazed

*"We all will celebrate and rejoice over You! We will sing with
praises our lyrics of Your better-than-wine love. It is no wonder
righteousness adores You!" (Song of Songs 1:4, TPT).*

The bystander and scientist will both be amazed at new findings
and unexplainable events mutually in the atmosphere and
deep under the earth. The news media will also embrace
this great wave of amazing and unexplained phenomenons being
reported. This does not mean that the secular media will also embrace
Christianity, in fact it will be quite the opposite. What will happen is
that the world will be amazed at what takes place all over the earth.
This global atmospheric shifting will also force favor over hidden
inventions for Christians. There is a creative river flowing from the
throne onto God's people in abundance in this hour. Some of you
reading this have invented things that have lain dormant because it
was not yet time, and now is the time.

You must learn well in this coming season to come together and how
coming together as one changes the atmosphere over complete regions.
This is so vital in the years ahead because unity brings peace, and peace
will foster creativity. When God's presence is there, His power and
provision will manifest. Some of you have fallen under serious financial
devastation, and the solution is two fold:

(1) Gather His people to speak into the financial realms and take authority, calling forth funds from the heavens. It is the wealth of the kingdom that must be released. This can come through many avenues, but however it is done over your region, be in agreement with your co-laborers. Unity is a must in these circumstances. Prayer changes the atmosphere of your town and it can alter the affects of poverty for good. Poverty is a curse! Though it can be used to bring about God's divine plan in someone's life, it is not designed for the righteous. Develop a team in your community through your pastoral leadership in that region and come together and pray. Bring some key Christian business owners, pastors, and genuine networkers together and make something good begin to happen right there in your community. Why does the next community over have to have all the supplies and goods? Figure out how to make it happen in your community.

(2) Bring forth the prophets to speak over the land! Once you have done number one above, get some key prophetic voices to come into your region for the purpose of intercession and prophetic wisdom over your land. I don't believe that we just speak in money and poof—it is there. I will say that money is best created through the wisdom of Proverbs. My money has not come through wealthy inheritances or finding stolen money up in a tree. It has all come through God's grace and my family's extremely hard and patient work. The two powers (hard work and patience) work together when dealing with money. In fact, God will normally not allow you to handle millions until you have discovered the true value and ability to faithfully manage a few dollars here and there. When you are faithful in the small things that God allots to you, then and only then will God allow you to have an increase of God's abundance. All other roads will only lead to future devastation. There is no real quick path to getting money other than genuine rewards from God's throne.

What I am suggesting here is that you bring in a key prophet or two to see what God is saying about your land. This is not a crusade for large offerings or to get rich quick. That would not be the purpose. Of course, bring the prophets in after you have prepared the spiritual ground and developed a strong network of key leaders to handle this divine task of bringing forth financial provision in your land. You can't walk alone and you certainly can't do this alone, so don't try. Remember, "Many advisors bring success" (Proverbs 15:22).

I am so serious about this that the company I own is actually setting up its own distribution system for creative and inventive (all original) ideas and products. If you or someone you know is a Christian and you are looking to get your idea or product out on the market you can personally contact me and we will see what can be done to help you meet your goals (www.5foldmedia.com).

As in the Days of Moses

"Then the Lord told him, 'I have certainly seen the oppression of
my people in Egypt. I have heard their cries of distress because
of their harsh slave drivers. Yes, I am aware of their suffering'"
(Exodus 3:7).

Our nation has fallen right into the same trap of the Israelites and that is bondage. We have allowed "foreign gods" to come into our sacred land and desecrate it. We have stopped prayer in schools and now we have guns. We have stopped Bible teachings in public sectors and now we have drugs. We can't pray in certain public circles or even have a manger scene out during Christmas at the town hall. In return for this we have religious and radical groups now coming in to our towns from all over parts of the world and destroying our sacred land and replacing it with evil idols and practices. In addition to this, our government has turned a blind eye in helping the righteous, yet they have opened their hearts freely to helping the wicked prosper. Unless it turns quickly, this nation is going to crumble, just like in the days of Moses, when Israel rested in the power of Pharaoh.

We can no longer call this country blessed when sin is rampant at all levels of this nation from the White House to the cornfields. From coast to coast there is an urgent need for the Christian to stand up and shout out the truth. This country is in dire need of a true Moses, one who is called to deliver God's people once again. I can say that God is not concerned as much with a nation that calls themselves a Christian nation as much as a person that calls themselves a Christian believer. If God was looking for a nation to have them corporately worship Him, He would have kept the same procedures like He had back in the days of Moses. No, He is looking for an individual, a people, if you will, that will stand up on their own for the truth and the love of God. This nation might be crumbling, but your spirit does not have to. This nation's government might be in bad trouble, but your life does not have to be directed and dictated by a temporal system. God wants you to grow in and through His kingdom right now, regardless of what is going wrong around you.

Like in the days of Moses, God is looking for a man or woman of God to stand up and fight for His people—one who will stand up to the evil powers of this land and speak the truth with divine signs and wonders to follow.

God, send us a prophet to our capital. Send us a prophetic voice to every single government leader in this nation. Release a supernatural encounter over every political figure and person that has any say into the governing laws of this land. In Jesus' name. Amen!

IV

Cleansing and Purity

The Man in the Mirror

"So please, my lord, let me (Judah) stay here as a slave instead of the boy, and let the boy return with his brothers" (Genesis 44:33).

"Then he (Joseph) broke down and wept. He wept so loudly the Egyptians could hear him, and word of it quickly carried to Pharaoh's palace" (Genesis 45:2).

In this season of Joseph's life and the preceding chapters, Joseph tested his brothers to see if they had really changed, and indeed they had. At the sight of seeing his brothers, who once had betrayed him and now were not willing to betray the youngest brother, Joseph could no longer control himself. The brothers had changed! They had repented and in their hearts had vowed to never let it happen again. This is real change, and this is what a dream that I recently had points out:

In the dream, there was a man who stood in the mirror gazing at every point of his life. In time, the mirror began to expose real life and very serious sins within him that God had been attempting to deal with for years. Overwhelmed with conviction and a desire to change, the man could not bear it any longer. The room suddenly went dim. The man in the mirror could no longer see a single sin in his life. While the room was still dim, the man stepped to his left side. His determination to leave the sins crushed the chains of bondage and entanglements that held him for so long. The cords were permanently broken. After this, he was a changed man and free, not bound by the reoccurring strongholds that kept coming back over and over again. Everyone noticed a major difference in his life from that day on.

What is this saying? God will give us strength to face our weaknesses (mirror and stepping out on the left side) and for this reason we will be changed. Reoccurring temptations that we have battled for decades without victory will be broken off. It is time for the Lord to take the broom and sweep out our spiritual closets. It is also time to take a look in the mirror and really allow God to show us what we need to change. Too often it is not the person next to you that is the problem, it is the person in you that needs to be adjusted.

The Fire

"Seek the Kingdom of God above all else, and live righteously, and he will give you everything you need" (Matthew 6:33).

"Sing a new song to the Lord! Sing his praises from the ends of the earth! Sing, all you who sail the seas, all you who live in distant coastlands" (Isaiah 42:10).

The great fire filled the entire earth as a symbol of purity and a true shaking at every level on each continent. As the fire burned strong, under the surface of the earth rose hands of all shapes, colors, and sizes. The hands created music. Each hand beat at first with its own rhythm on something like a small drum. Each drum represented a different culture or race. As the fire grew more intense, the little drummer hands played with more strength and beat closer in time with the other drummers all over the world. The fire brought the hands to complete unison, and these young worshippers created amazing, heavenly sounds. All the sounds were new because much of the old was burned up in this stronger and less compromising holy flame. This is a fire that ushers in unity—through worship—in the people of God. Unity is birthed in the fire as one person learns to overcome another person's faults. This is the place where genuine "David and Jonathan" friendships are formed.

What goes into these fires will be the bad things that never previously fell off of us (and in some cases, out of us) during the shakings on the earth. God is purging us and allowing us to come clean before we stand in His mighty presence one day. There are coming some of the worst natural fires in the history of this earth. When? I don't know. Not only will the land be hit by some of the most devastating fires ever seen before, it will also run parallel with a new fresh fire of God that will not only baptize us with a new and stronger fire, it will also cause us to get the junk out of our lives. God's holy fire will burn the dross out of our lives. There is sin in some camps and it is time to come clean. Time for some more fire in your life!

The Plumb Line Has Fallen

*"I will judge Jerusalem by the same standard I used for Samaria
and the same measure I used for the family of Ahab. I will wipe
away the people of Jerusalem as one wipes a dish and turns it
upside down" (2 Kings 21:13).*

In a vision, a plumb line swung across the skies. I heard the Lord say, "I am weighing and measuring for a house of purity." Then I saw three visions fall down out of the sky in front of me:

The first vision passed by and there were politicians falling on their faces before God in genuine prayer, being interrupted by sovereign and unscheduled moves of God. Obviously, if there is any region in the United States that needs more spiritual cleaning, it is indeed Capital Hill. This is the one area that must have constant intercession around the clock. How can we say that America is blessed if the government continues to openly allow blatant sin to be signed into law as it has been? God cannot bless sin! I will say that there is a difference between a government under judgment and a people being blessed. God's people are blessed because we choose to follow Him, regardless of what our government does. In addition to these thoughts, a country may not be blessed due to sin in the government, but it still has God's grace over it. I believe that this is the case for the United States. Sin is in the camp for sure, but God's grace is also stronger than any sin being offered. God has not lifted His grace off of America!

The second vision was of government leaders standing up and repenting. Many of these politicians went to their enemies and made it right, not because they had to, but because they knew it was the right thing to do. "Political repentance" will be released! Will all government officials do this? No! But you will see some start to make some things right before congress and before the television cameras. God will turn His conviction toward Capitol Hill and send forth His mantle of forgiveness to those who receive it. For those that don't, it will get really bad for them.

In the last vision, there was a politician speaking at a political event and the Holy Ghost took over and he went from speaking to preaching the Word of God. God will move some in this government from "politician" to "child of God." Many unplanned events are on the horizon for government leaders and now is the time to lift them up in prayer and also remind them that they are in a very prominent and powerful position on earth. It is a career that influences every major and minor country on earth by the decisions they make. Not only are they to be held accountable to those who voted them in, they are held accountable by God.

I believe that this vision of the plumb line and the three political visions that followed it represent the Obadiahs of our time. These are people that serve under wicked leaders and are willing to stay hidden, but at the same time, house the prophets in order to preserve the presence of God's people within the land. Obadiah had fifty prophets in one cave and fifty in the other, yet at the same time was working directly for Ahab, a most wicked king. Why did Ahab keep him around? Because God allowed Obadiah's work ethic to find favor with Ahab, and God also hid the secret work Obadiah was doing on the side. These are the days we are living in and the prayers that need to go up to God for the White House is that He bring in and rise up these Obadiahs to take care of and protect the Christians that remain here in America.

The Plumb Line Has Fallen

These visions also represent purity that I believe will strike some individuals at Capitol Hill. If there is any place on earth that needs purification right now, it is the White House as well as our individual hearts. You may not be able to have control of what goes on anymore in the White House, but you sure can be in control of what is allowed to happen within your own heart. Make sure you pray for this nation and the leaders, and also make sure that you keep a pure and clean heart, because that is what will keep you on course for one of the greatest times one could ever have in this nation.

Complacency is the Enemy's Best Weapon

"Honor and majesty surround him; strength and joy fill his dwelling" (1 Chronicles 16:27).

God is saying, "Complacency has been the enemy's plan to stop My efforts to send a global outpouring. The enemy has attempted to choke some of you out one centimeter at a time. The solution is to gather together to worship Me. This will kill complacency in your regions. It is time to regroup and gather to fight. Come together more and more. I have the enemy right where I want him, and I will use your gatherings to bring him down and be replaced by My seed. I will use the tactics of the enemy that were set against you to bring the enemy down and debunk his own plans. I will use you to gather, pray, and fight to win every case, battle, and territory. No more lost territory. Now is the time to gather and pray.

"The enemy has set out traps of complacency. I say in this hour, snap off those cords of complacency. Complacency is the cousin of confusion! Move out by the Spirit. When you move your feet, cords cannot entangle you. It is when you stop moving your feet that cords can be wrapped around your ankles."

I have had the privilege over the years to meet very prominent people and be able to listen to how they got started or what events transpired in their lives to help forge them into who they are today. I am always fascinated to hear these stories and stand amazed every time. The way God destines a path for a person is absolutely astonishing.

Most of the success stories I hear revolve around a handful of reasons for the accomplishments. Obviously, first and foremost is God. He is in control and can make anything happen. Then right after that comes a couple more reasons that I hear on a regular basis linked with success. Surprisingly, many would think here that it would be someone who inherits large amounts of money, like one born into royalty. Actually, in today's wealth patterns it is usually the exact opposite. I often find that a blend of determination, research, and hard work are what God uses to turn someone's life around. All of these biblical foundations for success are enemies of complacency.

Let's bring this into more light. Suppose someone was given a garden to oversee when they were young. This individual had a few choices at that moment. One choice would be to just let it go and then sell or destroy it. Another choice would be to study gardening, cultivate it well each year, and make a return, thus producing something. Sounds like common sense doesn't it? Too many times the gardens of our lives turn into very little because we failed to have determination, do the research, and work hard within the cycles of our seasons. The fact is, poverty is a curse and it is not from God. The other truth to poverty is oftentimes the patterns that got someone into poverty are the same nasty patterns that keep them there. Poverty does not always have to happen, and in some cases it is out of that person's control. I refuse to accept that everyone joining the welfare lines these days can't go out and find work or do something with their lives. In order to snap the chains of poverty, you must deal first with the cords of complacency. Poverty and complacency are kissing cousins.

Hidden Agendas

"The Lord of Heaven's Armies has spoken—who can change his plans? When his hand is raised, who can stop him?" (Isaiah 14:27).

The enemy's "stealth operations" will be exposed in this coming era. Many hidden agendas will be uncovered for the world to see. Relating to the government powers that are not aligning themselves with the Lords work, what was whispered in private will be yelled on the rooftops. Exposing a plan is hard to accomplish sometimes, but it can be done. The enemy's stealth fighters are not invincible and neither are the plans of the enemy. Let's parallel this concept to modern-day stealth technology:

Stealth aircraft are aircraft that use stealth technology to avoid detection by employing a combination of features to interfere with radar as well as reduce visibility in the infrared, visual, audio, and radio frequency (RF) spectrum. Development of stealth technology likely began in Germany during World War II. While no aircraft is totally invisible to radar, stealth aircraft prevent conventional radar from detecting or tracking the aircraft effectively, reducing the odds of a successful attack.

At long range, the stealth could possibly be detected because of reflected radar waves, infrared or heat, or various types of advanced radar systems. Stealth aircraft are still vulnerable to detection during and immediately after using their weaponry.

The only time that a stealth aircraft had been shot down was on March 27, 1999, during Operation Allied Force. An American F-117 Nighthawk fell to a Serbian Air Defense crew who were operating their radars on unusually long wavelengths to launch a Isayev S-125 'Neva-M' missile at it which brought it down. The pilot ejected and was rescued and the aircraft itself remained relatively intact.

A B-2 crashed on February 23, 2008 shortly after takeoff from Andersen Air Force Base in Guam. The findings of the investigation stated that the B-2 crashed after "heavy, lashing rains" caused water to enter skin-flush air-data sensors, which feed angle of attack and yaw data to the computerized flight-control system. The water distorted pre-flight readings in three of the plane's 24 sensors, causing the flight-control system to send an erroneous correction to the B-2 on takeoff. The B-2 quickly stalled, became unrecoverable, and crashed.[3]

As you can see, the stealth aircraft is a magnificent machine— definitely up there as the top of the line. Yet, these fierce fighting machines are vulnerable because they were created by humans in a fallen world. This is also the case with the enemy's plans against the Lord's people. The plans may be perfect in idea and design, but they are not flawless when carried out.

The enemy has grown smarter over the years. There is an old saying that says: "Give a fool a long enough rope and they will eventually hang themselves." We are dealing with high profile criminals now and they are getting really good at what they do, which is creating more impacting crimes. Yes, you do have to be concerned with the thug that attempts to break into your garage to steal some tools. You also now have to be greatly concerned with the little kid on his computer in another country that just hacked into your account and has passed your information around the world by the click of one button. Likewise, what is going on behind the scenes in government offices around the world would probably cause us all to cry if we really knew what was happening.

---

3. Wikipedia contributors, "Stealth aircraft," Wikipedia, The Free Encyclopedia, http://en.wikipedia.org/w/index.php?title=Stealth_aircraft&oldid=446370807 (accessed August 25, 2011).

"Cracks are forming in the enemy's plans against this nation and hidden agendas will start to crumble." There are some very bad things going on right now in this country and against it. Just about two minutes of news is all one can nearly take these days and the mainline news channels are not even sharing half of the facts and truth. Can you imagine what is really going on now behind closed doors?

Not all that is planned against our wonderful country will come to pass because it is not God's perfect will. I would also like to add that people who have plans to damage this country will be caught. These individuals will help bring down some within their own criminal networks. God does not condone the sin in this country and government, but He is not done with America either. He will see to it that the enemy is exposed and that His truth will prevail over this land.

Evil Will Rise Against Evil

"When the 300 Israelites blew their ram's horns, the Lord caused
the warriors in the camp to fight against each other with their
swords" (Judges 7:22).

Broken international treaties among the wicked will surface more and more as the new order of government settles further. We are now living in a land that is quickly turning from good to very evil, and fast. It is a new era for sure. What you and I must understand now is that the wicked have no rules. This means that if they need more cash or someone gone, they will deny, lie, steal, or in some cases even create a rule just to destroy something that is in their way. The cravings of the wicked never end. They hunger for more and more. They are willing to kill and destroy at all cost. For this reason, watch how the unrighteous will turn on the unrighteous. God is sending diversions now to the enemy. This is going to force the enemy to be distracted and turn on their own. Remember in gang activity and high-profile politics, one only has another person's back as long as they are needed, and everyone eventually becomes expendable. Once someone is no longer needed, in these two circles, they are normally found washed up on some riverbank somewhere. All said, when greed hits the heart of a wicked person, they will stop at nothing to get the job done. When this time comes, it is like a vicious dog fight, and that is what is brewing on the horizon for some.

When God uses the winds to turn evil against evil it is the "Spirit and wisdom in the same manner of Gideon." God will intentionally create situations to force the wicked to turn their efforts away from the righteous and back onto the wicked. This will create a season of regathering and rearming for the body of Christ. It is a window of time to remobilize, allowing the believers to unite and gain strategy. It is time to have a strong plan before going into the next years ahead. It is time to move forward.

Discerning Good from Evil

"A prudent person foresees danger and takes precautions.
The simpleton goes blindly on and suffers the consequences"
(Proverbs 22:3).

In a recent dream, a man was driving a truck and pulled over to stop for a moment. It was a very clear, sunny day. A young teenage girl came up to the man while he was standing outside and said, "I need to get a ride to the next town to see my boyfriend." Shocked, the man said, "Young girl, don't you realize how dangerous this is? You don't even know me and how do you know I am not some person that would hurt you?" Her response was saddening, "I desperately need to get to the next town to see my boyfriend. I want to see him that bad." (Then I instantly woke up.)

The young girl was so passionate about her own desires that she failed to see the danger that she was willing to put herself in. This is a picture of what must change now. Some in the body of Christ, if not careful, will digress into a lack of discernment. When personal passions take the place of common sense in our society, we are then in big trouble. How will this epidemic be stopped? It will be stopped by getting into the Word of God and into your own private prayer closet. Some reading this have been placed into dreadful situations, and in some cases, it is not all God's fault. In some situations, it is a direct result of a lack of serious common sense and discernment. We can allow God to mature us through learning how to operate in the Spirit while walking in the natural. In the dream, the young girl did not care about how she got to her boyfriend's location as long as she got there to see him. She was willing to put her own life at risk for something that, more than likely, was just a temporal relationship and that one day would eventually end. This is the state of some within our churches these days. Don't fall victim to the lack of self-control and the void of discernment.

Heresy happens when we place our personal revelation in a higher priority than God's written Word. There are some things in life you really do not have to prophesy about because it is already written in God's Word and it will happen. I was in a meeting once where a well-known prophet rebuked the spirit of the antichrist off the earth for good. This was just plain ignorant, because it goes against what the Bible says will happen in the last days. Sadly, there are those in the church who will believe this can happen. These types of heretical teachings only breed confusion.

Seven Times Hotter

*"I have come to bring fire on the earth, and how I wish it were
already kindled!" (Luke 12:49).*

As the ironworker forged the sword, he shouted out the command, "Turn up the heat seven times hotter." The short, hardworking ironworker was crafting a very precious sword. As he stood next to the hot iron kettle, he noticed that this sword was unique, unlike any he had made before. In fact, the normal temperature in the blazing fire pit would have done the job, but for this specific sword, the owner needed it stronger than in times past. Right beside the worker's shop stood an extremely tall mountain. It was God's mountain. The sweaty ironworker looked upward and said to the glorious mountain that stood beside him, "Turn it up. Turn it up seven times hotter." The Lord then increased the flames seven times hotter. During this time, the sword was finished and given to its owner. The owner of the sword is the Lord. The sword has been precisely ordered for the body of Christ now. The problem is low spiritual heat and fire. Now is the time to turn up the heat! As the heat increases on this earth, burning away all that does not belong, so will the glory of God increase in the hearts of His people. Remember, heat burns but it can also comfort and protect on a deep and dark snowy night. This world is going deeper into sin, yet the Holy Ghost will be the Comforter for all who will allow His gracious protection as this world gets darker.

Later in that same dream, everything on earth was tested and purified. Finally, a beautiful bride was strong enough to handle the precisely engineered sword. What will come out of this stronger flame? This is simple: A bride that has made herself ready for Jesus and His great return. Jump into this spiritual fire and burn bright for Him.

V

Touch the World

Go After the Schools

"But Jesus said, 'Let the children come to me. Don't stop them! For the kingdom of heaven belongs to those who are like these children.'" (Matthew 19:14).

In a dream, two opposing forces both jumped into the nation's schools at the same time and began to battle for the souls and minds of our nation's children. The strongest attempts to take school territory by both the righteous and the wicked are here right now. Both forces are colliding on school properties all over the nations. The enemy will do anything possible to destroy the foundation of Christianity in our young people. The government, unfortunately, has made tougher laws to attempt to block Christian groups from being involved in any way inside the school systems. This may be a growing problem, but it should not stop us for good.

Turn school meetings back to God. Take the leadership roles this next season when key spots open up for voting. It is urgent to push back the enemy and draw lines to protect the future of our nation. Use key seats and volunteer positions in your school districts to implement sound and commonsense vision. With all the humanistic and Marxist ideologies moving into our school systems, there is an extreme lack of rational thinking and the ability to take the lead. This means that most, if not all of our districts are understaffed and under volunteered at the same time. Use this to your advantage to get into the school systems to help out. Once you are in there, ask the Lord to show you what He would have you do to touch people. Remember, when you are in a public school you are under their rules so always ask before you do anything.

Shortly after this dream, my wife and I went to a school PTA meeting and then a school board meeting. I found the leaders of our school system to be very levelheaded and stable in many ways. They don't appear at this time to buy into all the federal rules that are being passed down from Capitol Hill right now. For the most part, we were impressed with how this school leadership functions. Anyway, we noticed how desperately they were looking for helpers. Volunteers were needed at just about every level of the school system. I would guess that this would be about the same in your school district, being that the government keeps cutting school funding, yet raising property taxes. What does this mean for you? It means that you have a golden opportunity now to get into the school systems that you probably did not have just a decade ago.

After the Columbine High School massacre, most of the districts closed their doors on everyone wanting to help out in the schools, deeming every person a serious threat. I don't blame the school districts for doing that. I think it was a wise idea. Besides, you can't tell anymore who is wanting to kill you or actually wanting to help you these days! This problem is the same with school kids. That is what was so frustrating with Columbine because the bad kids looked just like the good ones. A seemingly normal and stable child can easily show up with a gun and this seems to be happening more and more.

What is occurring now is that our school systems are falling apart. There are not enough funds to keep everything up to date in our schools anymore. For this reason, volunteers are greatly needed. Use this opportunity to go make an impact in the schools. This little window of opportunity will not be around forever. In fact, it is slowly closing again.

Slave Trade Industry

"But their evil intentions will be exposed..." (Ephesians 5:13).

I had a dream where a young, attractive lady was taken. She was forced into the sex slave industry for a brief time. Within moments she was able to escape by the help of some people that I have never seen before. The Lord then spoke immediately about how these people are the ones who will dismantle the sex trade industry. They were hidden, low-profile Christians.

In the dream, freeing the victims happened so fast. These plain-clothed individual teams were in and out with the rescues and were able to get the victims into safe recovery systems. In addition to quicker rescues, the young lady who was taken gave vital information to these "secret Christian rescue teams" about what was really going on and how this industry can be brought down. While watching this in the dream, I heard the Spirit say, "I am going to leak vital information out about this industry. I am going to cut off some of the trade routes by natural disasters." We are entering into an era that will bring exposure over this wicked industry.

I personally believe that this is going to become one of the most vital ministries of the local church. Why? I don't believe the government can truly make a huge dent into these sex slave organizations because I personally think some within our governments are actually involved.

That's right, making a profit off of innocent kids. Now, don't get me wrong here, I don't believe every government leader or even every government is a part of this wicked industry. I believe there are some dotting different parts of the world here and there and this is what is going to make it hard to kill out this industry. For this reason, it is vital for the local church to come together and create another "underground railroad." Just like back in the days where white people all over this nation risked their lives and families to house and protect black slaves, we, as Christians, are going to need to do the same thing again in order to rescue sex slave victims. These victims will have to be protected long after they are recovered because the leaders in the industry will not be willing to get caught or found out for any reason. They will go to any extreme to stay hidden and profit from this detestable industry.

There are ministries and all kinds of organizations popping up all over this world to assist in freeing sex slaves and putting a stop to sex trafficking. If your church or ministry group is not involved with helping to free sex slave kids, please get involved. Sex slavery is unlike black slavery, which had primarily attacked the black and African race. Sex slavery affects every color and race of children all over the world. Unfortunately, we too often tend to forget that slavery has not actually stopped in the United States; it has just turned into many colors and is now affecting every major city of this nation.

God is calling some of you who are reading this to lay aside your own desires, and start developing a plan for how you are going to make an impact into this evil industry. Some reading this have already had dreams, prophetic words, and other confirmations as to your calling to recapture these innocent victims.

If you are a part of one of these organizations I would personally like to know more about how you are helping to stop this industry. Please email me at: andy@5foldmedia.com. I would like to talk with you to see how we can help.

The Underground Church Doors Will Open

"God knows people's hearts, and he confirmed that he accepts Gentiles by giving them the Holy Spirit, just as he did to us. He made no distinction between us and them, for he cleansed their hearts through faith" (Acts 15:8-9).

The hatches of the underground church will open in many areas over the next decade. For too long the saints have been hidden. The Lord says, "Many of My global kingdom generals are sitting hidden and physically starving in the underground networks in Asia, Russia, and the Middle East. I am opening the hatches of some of these networks to release many generals in order to train other cultures how to battle and win. In a day's time some of these underground kingdom generals will be released.

"I am releasing the tactics I taught to the underground church to be taught to the 'above ground' church. I am going to fuse together the passions and callings of both the 'above ground' and 'underground' churches. The two of you have been like independent children up to this moment, in many cases acting as if you do not even know of or need each other. You will learn the power of becoming one over these new seasons of your lives. I will show you how to love and care for each other as a brother to a brother. During this coming era, you will begin to discover that everyone in My house really needs each other."

Gather the Flocks and the Harvest

"But I will gather together the remnant of my flock from the countries where I have driven them. I will bring them back to their own sheepfold, and they will be fruitful and increase in number"
(Jeremiah 23:3).

Over the next several months as you place an importance in corporate gatherings and worship, it will force a global shift in the atmosphere on earth. As this shift takes its shape, it will also create signs and wonders in the natural atmospheres around the earth.

God will place a strong emphasis on the corporate level and how it will affect the outflow of His anointing to Christians. We, as believers, must come together and learn to start meeting each other's needs. How will this take place? One way will be through worship. I believe God will start laying His deep power on people as they worship. Expect amazing outbreaks of God's mighty Spirit to move on people as they come together and worship. Another way is through discernment. We must use discernment to show us where we will put our time and resources in these last days. We cannot do everything all the time, but can do some here and there. Knowing what field to sow into with our time and money is very important right now.

We are no longer living in an era where church or Christian gatherings are an option. Now and in the years ahead, we will desperately need each other to not only stay alive but stay bonded together through the power of God's love. In the past, missing gatherings was okay, in many ways. Besides, most were boring and what did we have to fear or lose? We could just go to church or the next big event in a few more days. This will not be so in the future of this nation. It is going to be harder and harder to worship God and preach the true Word of God without government manipulation. Imagine in a few more decades what it will be like? My point here is: as Christians we are obligated to come together. This is going to become an important aspect of our lives in the coming days, and if not, it will harm our relationships in the long run. The harvest will increase as we learn to spend more time with the Lord and with each other. Real maturity comes when an individual could easily leave their church because of an offense but instead chooses to stay and work it out.

Power Over the Cities

"'Well done!' the king exclaimed. 'You are a good servant. You have been faithful with the little I entrusted to you, so you will be governor of ten cities as your reward'" (Luke 19:17).

The cities will change as the power seats of the regions shift. For too long the wrong people have had some of the right seats of influence. As a believer, one can no longer sit back, pray, and just hope. We must pray, hope, and march forward. America will be won by taking the community one step at a time. Find the seats of influence and fill them in this coming year. When you take the seats of influence in the community, you have God-given governmental authority to control the direct effects of what is going in and out of your city.

Christianity is a complete way of life that must affect every level of our community. One cannot be a Christian without having the presence of Christ manifest in everything around them, including the government. Purity in a city starts on the foundation of prayer and repentance. Pure change within a region comes through taking important seats of power that can activate pure and healthy decisions over that region.

We are no longer living in a country where Christians can just sit back and let the "good ole" politicians righteously lead our nation. Christians must become active in every level of our government—from the school boards all the way to the president of the United States. We need true and genuine leaders to come and take our land back. That, my friend, starts with you and me. You may be asking, "What can I do?" Well, for starters you can get involved by showing up to town hall meetings, school board meetings, or even participate in local rallies. My wife and I went to a school board meeting once to sit in and were amazed at just how much the school was desperately seeking volunteer help. As a result, we have gotten involved more over the years. In addition to this, we are in the process of getting more involved with our community. Why? The schools and communities we all live in need God-fearing leaders to stand in the gap and protect our local areas from sinful decisions that are being passed down through our higher-level governments. What has happened is that the key leaders and positions in our nation have now been usurped by ultra-liberal ideologies. This will only trickle down in time, unless it is completely stopped. Don't just depend on your neighbor or your pastor to do this type of work. Get involved before the wrong person in your community does.

I look at it this way, if you get involved and take a key seat in your region, then you now have government authority to make righteous decisions. If someone with evil intentions takes the seat that you could have (and should have) had in the first place, then that person has the authority to make wicked decisions for you and your household. Don't let this happen anymore. Get involved! Do something while you still can.

VI

Prophetic Revelation

The Bride

"Instead, he (Christ) gave up his divine privileges; he took the
humble position of a slave and was born as a human being. When
he appeared in human form, he humbled himself in obedience to
God and died a criminal's death on a cross" (Philippians 2:7-8).

This dream came on the night of my birthday. It is a beautiful picture of God's love for His bride and the prophet's responsibility to speak, honor, and take care of her. We are to offer God's children a true word with a selfless love. There is a crossroads on earth, and it is imperative for the prophets to offer a lifestyle that puts their needs aside for the duty to nurture God's people. (Note: in Scripture, a king represents Jesus or God. A bride represents the bride of Christ. You will notice in this dream that the unfulfilled bride was looking for help [love] from a husband. The husband here represents the leadership of the church.)

The setting of this dream alternated between modern day and the age of kings and queens. There was a young prophet in a room with a princess, and suddenly a lot of kids and younger teenagers entered the room. The kids were going to pack up and go to a worship center located in Kansas—representing a place of intimate prayer transformation. The children expected the young prophet to help them pack, and they were leaving in just a few days. Having the prophet help them pack was not God's plan. God wanted the young children to learn to pack and prepare for their own journeys, taking responsibility for what they were called to do. So, the prophet did not pack the young kids' bags for them. He left it up for them to decide just how badly they wanted to get to Kansas. If they wanted to get there then they would be willing to prepare on their own.

In the meantime the princess (the king's daughter) said that she was going on a journey to find a man who will love her for who she was. She was supposed to have a different person take her on this journey, and it fell through. This sad announcement was told outside and before all the town people right in front of the king. Once the sad announcement took place, the young prophet bowed down to the king and said, "I will take your daughter to help her find a man." The young daughter looked directly at the young prophet, and then the prophet stood up. She showed the prophet her left ear, and it looked normal except with a slight yellowish color right near the inner ear. Her ear was slightly wounded but was in the healing process. She said, "And this is how I will know: The man that loves me will rub my left ear for two whole months." The young prophet thought, *How gross!* The young man then said to her, "Don't you think that is strange and gross?" The princess said, "And this is how I shall know that this man loves me because this is what he will do for me. He will rub his right index finger in my ear, close to my inner ear, and on the yellow spot for two whole months. This is how I shall know this man loves me." The young prophet stood there speechless for the first time in his life. Can you imagine a prophet actually speechless? He realized many would come and be tested by this, and then many men would leave. This bride was determined to encounter the real love of her life and this decree would be the final test. To be willing to rub someone's ear for two months, that person would really have to love them!

At this time, the king looked at the young prophet and said, "It is good. Take my daughter to find her husband who will love her the way she wants to be loved. You will leave in two days. She will have her ear rubbed for two whole months, and you will return in exactly two years." The king took his left hand, placed it in his left pocket, and pulled out about seven or eight golden coins. Each coin was the same rounded shape and size, but each was different in thickness. The young prophet first thought, *That is not enough for the two years to cover all of our travels. The king could give more than this. This is the king's daughter, and that is it?* At the end of the two years, however, the entire caravan returned. When the young prophet looked back, he realized that what the king had actually given was far more valuable than he could imagine because it was right from the king's hand and forged only for him and his family. For this reason, there was an abundance of favor and wealth during this trip with more than enough provision and still plenty left over at the end.

Let's Discuss a Few Items Here:

1. *Children getting ready to go to Kansas.* I don't believe this is just a physical place in Kansas as it obviously represents nonstop worship. God is calling the alignment and positioning of the nonstop worshipers over these next two years. Within these next two years, there will be pockets of full-time, nonstop worshipers established to settle into the lands of the earth and position themselves just to worship. This will create a stronger foundation for deep and extremely personal prophetic power to be loosed on the body of Christ. God has a lot to say over these next two years, giving clear direction in all realms of society. Worshipers, it is time to take the lead and open the gates of glory.

2. *The left ear, yellow spot, and close to the inner ear parts were to be rubbed for two months.* This area of the ear is the final entrance for sound to travel into the mind and be understood. Rubbing her ear was the only method that showed the king's daughter just who was really willing to love her for who she was and not for what he could get from her. This is a deep call to prophets (and leaders) to arouse the sounds of heaven for the body of Christ. This princess (the bride of Christ) is desperate for a personal touch of love from the Father. It is time for the elders of the land to rub the bride's ear and stir up that intimate, deep compassion for a completely fulfilled bride. The test showed who was and was not willing to please the bride of Christ and the one who showed worthy was the one who got the prize. The yellow spots represent past wounds in the prophetic circles now being healed. When someone is wounded by false prophets and false prophecy, they tend to shut out the

supernatural. Rubbing her wounded ear represents the body of Christ getting healed up, and then being aroused by genuine prophetic truth once again.

3. *Gold coins and two years.* This represents the fact that God will cover the cost for this journey many of you are about to take over the next two years. Much of the funding will be the supernatural release of God's favor on your lives. It will come through many natural and unexpected venues. You will look back and see that this coming journey to help heal and love the bride will be far more rewarding than anyone can see right now. The body of Christ will be so much more mature by the time we get to the end of this next season. It will be as if we have grown several years through this process because we decided to please the bride, thus honoring the King.

The Face of God

"Let us be glad and rejoice, and let us give honor to him. For the time has come for the wedding feast of the Lamb, and his bride has prepared herself" (Revelation 19:7).

It is crucial in this hour to tend to the needs of the bride of Christ. As things change so much right now, many within the Christian community are feeling as though they are being pressed from all sides, from many new adversaries, at an increasing rate. Christians are being attacked daily now. Just a brief time ago in our nation, it was good and in some ways cool to be a Christian. Now, if you say you are a Christian in some circles you may be severally persecuted right then and there. God needs us to help the bride of Christ now more than ever before.

Through applying grace, love, and protection to the bride, God's face will shine more and more through our lives. Yes, we are to evangelize and meet the needs of the poor at all levels of our society, but what I am seeing now is that we have unfortunately neglected our own in exchange for helping others that might not really appreciate what was done. In a sense, if we are not careful we can actually throw our pearls among swine instead of among folks that will use the talents and gifts for the right reasons. My point to this section is not to slow down or stop missions and outreach efforts, but to increase the tender loving care and protection to the body of Christ right now. For our Christian communities to grow and be healthy, we must have strong bonds at every connection. In order to do this, we must learn how to protect every aspect and part of the body of Christ. This will allow the whole body of Christ to function exactly the way it was intended and designed to. Take a look at this imagery below:

A woman stood over the earth looking upward, engulfed by the glory that shined down from God. Part of her face was covered in a stone mask while the other side was gleaming so brilliantly that all the earth could see that this was the bride of God. As the light shined stronger and stronger, and as the bride drew closer and closer to God, the side of her face with the stone mask turned to a fine sandy power. After a while, the mask lost its ability to stick and therefore lost its impact to hide part of the bride's magnificent face. The stone mask dissipated into fine sand, and then vanishing into air as it fell slowly to the ground, the Lord's river washed away any remnant of it. This stone covering would never again touch His bride. Nothing was ever partial again in the body of Christ. One bride and one King! Her completely exposed face was the most beautiful appearance ever. Breathtaking, pure, whole, confident, steady, and peace loving are just a few of the words to describe her. If this is a small glimpse of what the body of Christ will look like, we are in for the greatest journey one could ever have.

As the bride stood tall and without the mask, she turned and looked into the eyes of the Lord. One of His eyes saw the entire world. Every single item that ever took place or ever will, the eye of the Lord looked over it. This image depicts how God sees the big picture in life. What we can't see, He does. The other eye of the Lord saw every person in the world. This shows how detailed and just how personal Jesus really is. He knows the hairs on your head and even called you by name before you were born. He is the all-seeing God who cares for you deeply.

"I am filling you right now with a new love for My bride. The old tough and rough skins are passing right now, and a new layer of love and compassion is being placed in and around your heart."

"How great you are, O Sovereign Lord! There is no one like you. We have never even heard of another God like you!" (2 Samuel 7:22).

Intimacy in Marriage

"She arises from her desert of difficulty loving and leaning into her Beloved! When I awakened you as you were feasting upon Me under the apple tree; I awakened your innermost being with travail of birth as you longed for more of Me" (Song of Songs 8:5, TPT).

For nearly a year now, I have been having reoccurring visions and dreams about a transparent fire hovering over satin bedroom sheets. This is the fire of intimacy coming back to the bedrooms between husbands and wives all over this world. God is releasing true and pure intimacy to the married husband and wife. "Some couples have been robbed of one of MY most precious gifts. This is the ability to re-create and enjoy unity at the same time." The Lord is reprogramming husbands and wives who have struggled with this area. "I will pour out creativity in the marriage bedrooms. I will create a new fire of love between those relationships that have gone cold."

God is releasing a holy and pure fire back on the Christian couples. He is rebonding the husband and wife in this new day. In some cases, the glues of love, passion, commitment, and respect have grown weak between the man and wife. It is time for the Lord's ultra super glue to be poured out on the strings that hold a married man and woman together.

As a manifestation of the pure passion being poured out over His families, many reading this will find a new wine of the Spirit both while you are sleeping in your beds and while you are together as a couple throughout the day. Signs and wonders will increase in the bedroom. The world has owned the bedroom for too long and God will be taking this back to its original biblical plan.

New Christian healing ministries will begin to open up that will deal with intimacy issues in marriage. New paradigms will be released to the local churches to educate and bring genuine freedom into the marriage about intimate relations. The Church will adapt new methods in implementing real results for this next generation. The world cannot produce holy intimacy; only God can. Schools cannot teach children about true intimacy the way the Bible can. It is now time to see the fire of God's passion come back to the bedrooms of our Christian married couples once again. It is time to allow His healing power to touch the marriage sins and problems within God's house and watch the miracles become a testimony to this lost world.

It is now time for the church to show the world how to have the most amazing and fascinating sex ever discovered between a man and a woman. Christians should be the ones who hold the key to pure love and passion in the sheets. We have been silent and ashamed to pass on sexual truth that comes straight from the Word of God. Let the fire come back to the bedroom once again!

Hidden Oil

"And I will give you treasures hidden in the darkness—secret riches. I will do this so you may know that I am the Lord, the God of Israel, the one who calls you by name" (Isaiah 45:3).

"For this is what the Lord, the God of Israel, says: There will always be flour and olive oil left in your containers until the time when the Lord sends rain and the crops grow again!" (1 Kings 17:14).

I saw an extremely damaged oil vase come up from the dirt of the earth. In my mind, it was way too damaged to ever be used again. I wasn't sure if it could even hold oil. As it came up through the earth, I thought that I would never see the oil that might have possibly been hidden deep within that badly damaged vase. However, in a moment's time, the cap came off and the entire area was filled with an aroma like no other. It was the smell of Jesus.

The oil vase began to tip, and the oil started pouring out. Once it touched a part of my body, my entire being felt its potent healing agents. The oil never stopped, it continued to flow out upon the earth, moving from city to city, nation to nation. Then the Lord spoke and said, "I don't throw anything away, I salvage it. I am opening the vase of salvaged oil (restoration) over My people in this season. I am the God of restoration." For this very moment, the Lord has reserved His most precious and hidden oil.

As the oil flowed out, the dirt from around my life started being pushed back by the living oil of God. Not only was the oil pushing dirt from around me away from the area, but the oil was also cleansing hidden areas of dirt from inside of me. Issues I did not realize I had were exposed and cleansed right then and there.

God removes the dirt in our lives to uncover the nutrients that are found in the hidden oil. I believe that there is a new era coming on His children and this earth that will be releasing an intense oil of restoration and reconciliation. It is an oil that says, "We will not throw them away; instead, we will salvage every one of them and restore them to their original purpose and destiny."

This oil is extremely strong in nutrients. It is potent to the enemy because it will give enough life to whatever it touches to raise back up the dead areas of our lives and bring a total renovation. When God puts his hands of restoration on a life, He completes it fully. Something restored often increases in value and beauty.

No More Relying on "Foreign" Oil...This Priceless Heavenly Oil Will Be Discovered in Every Nation!

"The orchards and fields of my people will yield bumper crops,
and everyone will live in safety. When I have broken their
chains of slavery and rescued them from those who enslaved
them, then they will know that I am the Lord" (Ezekiel 34:27).

The word *foreign* makes me think of traveling to another country or nation. The Lord is beginning to wean His people from "foreign" oil, both spiritually and physically. No more will you have to travel to another place from where you live to strike the richest spiritual oil deposit on earth! No longer will this oil you need to live by have to be shipped in! This priceless oil will begin to be discovered in every nation, and man will not be able to contain it or put it into barrels to sell! No man or nation will have a monopoly on this spiritual oil that is now beginning to surface throughout the earth!

This oil will flow uncontrollably, touching the elite in governments and filling the gutters of the streets of the world. This heavenly oil will be so potent that it will cause physical oil deposits beneath the earth to come to the surface in order to be found as the earth yields her increase into the kingdom. Some reading this word now may be sitting on an oil deposit right on their property that was not there yesterday.

Years ago I sensed in my spirit, with all of the shaking going on in heaven and in the earth, that earthquakes may very well be shifting oil deposits toward the surface of the earth in various places. The coast of California is one of the most active areas for earthquakes and, interestingly enough, that's also where most of the oil seeps are located. There are some good things being shaken into God's kingdom this hour, as well as bad things being shaken out!

"We now have this light shining in our hearts, but we ourselves are like fragile clay jars containing this great treasure. This makes it clear that our great power is from God, not from ourselves" (2 Corinthians 4:7).

I then looked into the inside of that vase. The Lord showed me that this oil was rich and purified with many nutrients because it had been hidden for such a long time, and it is now being released on His children once again. His oil restores because it was once damaged. This oil can mend because it was once torn apart. And best of all, this oil can reveal because it has been hidden.

Do you feel destroyed? Has this season of your life been torn apart? When others were being recognized, were you the one who remained hidden? This is your time.

"This hidden oil is for you," says the Lord. "Do not be afraid to allow this oil to touch every area of your life. I am going to heal and restore you to get you positioned and ready for the next moment I have ordained for your life. There is a new era coming; a era of the revelation of my oil," says the Lord. "I am going to stop up some of the enemy's paths. I am going to confuse the enemy both coming and going. I will also humiliate the oppressor and accuser that has risen up against My children."

May the Lord restore, mend, and reveal much grace and power over your lives this coming era!

Love Covers All

*"'In that day, I will answer,' says the Lord. 'I will answer the sky
as it pleads for clouds. And the sky will answer the earth with
rain. Then the earth will answer the thirsty cries of the grain,
the grapevines, and the olive trees. And they in turn will answer,
"Jezreel"—"God plants!" ' " (Hosea 2:21-22).*

In a recent dream, there was a man working at his desk. The entire room
was filled with projects, goals, and vision for the coming months. The
man was tired and overworked. It was late at night, a time when most
should have been sleeping. The desk light was placed right near him and
there was clutter all over his desk and in many spots of the room.

As this Christian worker was sitting at his desk, suddenly a bottle of
oil fell over on the worker's desktop. It spilled all over everything and
ran in all directions. It fell on important papers, rolled off the desk, even
flowing on books and important files that were stacked on the floor.
Everything that this man had worked so hard to produce was instantly
saturated by this oil. More oil came out of the jar than the jar itself could
hold. It was a miracle, to say the least.

The Lord spoke these words in this dream, "This is My servant and
he has taken work too far. I want a relationship with him much more
than his efforts to build something for Me. I spilled the oil on purpose. I
did this to get his attention and to redirect him to what is most important

in life. Now that I have him where he will listen to Me, I will teach him once again that it is love that I want to work into every aspect of a person's life, not projects and goals."

It is time to love and release. Some believers have become obsessed with working to help the Lord instead of yielding to spend time with Him. God will free up our time so that we can find precious time with Him. There is a season for rest ,and to many reading this right now, this season is way past due.

Find the Place Where You Belong

"As for Philip, an angel of the Lord said to him, 'Go south down the desert road that runs from Jerusalem to Gaza.' So he started out, and he met the treasurer of Ethiopia, a eunuch of great authority under the Kandake, the queen of Ethiopia. The eunuch had gone to Jerusalem to worship, and he was now returning. Seated in his carriage, he was reading aloud from the book of the prophet Isaiah. The Holy Spirit said to Philip, 'Go over and walk along beside the carriage'" (Acts 8:26-29).

Notice it says here to Philip to go to that carriage and walk along beside it. The Holy Spirit explicitly pointed out that particular carriage. What do you think might have happened if Philip did not fully pay attention to what God just told him? Philip might have gone to just any carriage and not that particular one. This, my friends, happens all the time in the body of Christ. God will often give us a calling to go and do something and we end up doing it half way because we failed to pay attention to a small detail that later became the premise for our exact location. God's promise and blessing at this time was not on any carriage, but it was on the only carriage that God pointed out. Had Philip not been paying close attention to the exact details of his assignment, he might have just pursued the first carriage that came along.

In addition to God telling him to go over to this carriage listed above, Philip was also instructed to walk along beside it. This meant that he was to get close to it, regardless of what it meant at the time, and stay on call until God would tell him otherwise.

Let's bring the two together by going the opposite direction first. In some cases, some might have seen this as a ministry to carriages from this moment on. "God called me to a carriage ministry because He told me to go to a carriage once and stay near it and out of that one carriage someone got saved." Isn't this so much like us church leaders? God gives us simple instructions and it works greater than we ever imagined and from that moment on we keep doing it the same exact way over and over again. This is all well and good, if that is what God really wants, but sometimes it is just an isolated event with a distinct, yet passing purpose that God needed to fulfill at the time.

If we are not careful, we can end up going to any carriage when we were supposed to be near the one God meant for us. Also, we can go to the right carriage but not stay long enough to see the promise and blessing fulfilled. Before you go, make doubly sure you hear the voice of God. In addition to both the above, we can too often make a long-term ministry out of something that was intended to be a distinct assignment for a season before moving on to something else.

It is imperative that we discern God's will at all times. Sometimes God might have you continue on in certain patterns or make a ministry of it. He does this all the time. This does not mean, however, that it has to happen for the rest of your life. Make sure you are where you are supposed to be and doing exactly what you are supposed to do.

A Letter to You from God

"God has given me the responsibility of serving his church by proclaiming his entire message to you. This message was kept secret for centuries and generations past, but now it has been revealed to God's people. For God wanted them to know that the riches and glory of Christ are for you Gentiles, too. And this is the secret: Christ lives in you. This gives you assurance of sharing his glory" (Colossians 1:25-27).

The Lord says, "I love you, but I am not sure that you truly understand what I really want to create within you. You understand the 'through you' part but you have not grasped the 'in you' understanding. I am more concerned with being in you, rather than working through you. I can work through anyone or anything. I don't need to work through you as much as I want to be in you. I can live anywhere, but I choose to dwell in you. Not everyone will allow Me into their life. I desire to be in your life on the inside more than I wish to be displayed through you on the outside. I want to increase in you much more than I long to work through you. In some aspects, you care more about Me working through you. I want you to be acquainted with and learn to live with Me in you. That is My highest priority over your life.

"I want to work in you first. Allow Me to work in you, My child, and do not worry about what goes on through you. Do not focus on being talented like others you see because looks can be deceptive. I want to work through you after you have learned to let Me in you. That means that I can change anything I want within you. That is what I desire first. My relationship with you is what I want more than you displaying Me for all to see. I am not a trophy that needs to be displayed; I am God, who needs no introduction.

"Seek Me first and My passions will become your passions. I have you right where I want you. I have never made a mistake in your life and I never will make a mistake in your future. Your life can be forever changed if you allow Me to be in you before I am through you. Trust Me in this and see if I do not change your entire life forever to be better than what you think you can make of it on your own. I will change your life if you allow Me to be a Husband to your heart. Allow Me to circumcise all of your heart. Permit Me to change everything I see fit to."

VII

Stories to Tell

Empty Graves

"Why does it seem incredible to any of you that God can raise the dead?" (Acts 26:8).

One by one the soil beneath their feet continued to shake and the plots within the old cemetery section rattled underground as though a mild earthquake was happening. With fire blazing in his eyes, the prophet continued to walk quickly through the older section of the cemetery. This particular area was so old that some of the headstones were knocked over and had been sitting there for decades. A few plots must have been there for more than a century, as the headings were now unreadable. The grass in this location was not kept up as well as the new area the young prophet had just entered into. While leaving the older section and now entering into the new, he paused, looked around, and then stepped roughly nine feet to his right. He looked down at the fresh dirt piled high over a brand new cemetery plot just laid with a headstone and many flowers. Indeed, this was one of the newest ones in the cemetery and a bit smaller than most of the rest in plot size.

"Raise, I said, Now!" The man shouted to the ground, pointing at the dirt. One explosion happened after the next. The ground shook harder and harder. Solid rock headstones fell over, some breaking apart as plots of land burst open. Boom! Graves just kept popping open like God Himself was opening soup with a can opener.

The prophet, with a holy vengeance in his voice and a violent anger towards death, stopped for a brief moment and stood watching all that the Lord had just done in that cemetery. Caskets were blown to pieces sitting there wide open. Smoke and dust filled the atmosphere. The rotten stench of eroded bodies hit the air then evaporated, changing into a sweet smelling fragrance that some later described as blossoming lilies. Cars and trucks passing by on the road next to the cemetery were wrecking into each other, distracted by the supernatural moment. Everyone was in total shock as graves opened right before their very eyes.

Bones flew up from six feet under and began to form into living beings again right in the air. Great grandmothers, uncles, mothers, daughters, and for some strange reason, even a dog that must have gotten buried with its owner in one of the caskets, began to form. Talk about amazing! Even some dead bugs snapped back together and took off flying again. A few trees in the distance that were once hit by lightening and falling apart dead, instantly formed back to normal. Everything started coming back to life with the sound of that one single command from the young prophet's voice.

People stood there just looking at themselves and gazing at each other as the corpses in the cemetery came to life. Some of these once-dead bodies fell to the floor and wept. Others came back screaming and smelling like sulfur for a split second before the smell dissipated. Some began to quote scripture after scripture about the heavens and the Lord God. One really stood out in the crowd. He was a short, stubby little man from Georgia who talked with a twang. He jumped up shouting, "What in God's creation just happened? Man, I look better now than I did before I died!" He then shouted to the crowds, "Hey, ya'll! My name is Billy! If you see my wife tell her that I'm back and looking better than ever!" The tattoos that this man once had were all gone, along with the pain he used to carry in his right knee. He was a rough person before becoming born again just a few years before he had been killed in a boating accident. His wife had remained single, not even thinking about remarrying so soon.

The prophet walked over to a small casket and knelt down beside it quietly praying for about twenty minutes. Sirens were blaring in the distance and helicopters traveled from afar. People were yelling in fright as they watched. Before their eyes, close to one hundred dead people had now come to life with flesh, bones, breath, and all. One elderly lady that came back to life got so excited that she started dancing around in circles right there in front of everyone. She was having so much fun that she forgot where to step and kaplunk! She fell right into an empty grave. She landed head first and was out cold for a few minutes. When she came to, all you could hear from the little old lady was echoing laughter as she shouted," I told you Jesus was real! I told you so! He is alive! Ha-ha-ha-ha. Who-whoa!" She just kept screaming at the top of her lungs from inside the empty grave. Her once cancer-ridden body was completely whole again without any signs of treatment or pain.

The fascinating part of this whole event was that the old, decayed clothing that the dead people had been buried in no longer fit them and had fallen off. At the same time, new and properly fitting clothing appeared on them. Nobody came back naked. Not one. It was like God dressed them in thin air. Their new clothes fit perfectly!

The prophet pointed to a young couple, their faces as white as ghosts, and said to them, "Come here!" They walked slowly, shoulder to shoulder, as tight as they could toward the bold prophet. They walked through exploded grave sites, decayed clothing, dirt, and God only knows what else. The couple got to the little burial place that was one of the newest plots, based on the looks of the other headstones. Along with this being a fresh grave, it was smaller than normal, indicating that a very young child had been placed here. "Is this the one?" he said with a smile. "Um…yes!" the young girl said softly, her entire body shaking and still in shock. The young man next to her nodded, tears brimming in his eyes and running down his face. He was so scared he nearly passed out twice just standing near the prophet.

The presence of God was so strong in that cemetery that others later reported that they could hear even more dead graves starting to come alive and heavenly music playing in the background through open air speakers. What was really wild is that there were never any speakers or open air events reported within a forty mile radius from this cemetery on that day.

God's Spirit was radiating everywhere supernaturally. All of a sudden, the prophet jumped up and down on top of the little burial plot. The young couple nearly collapsed together in a state of shock. The young lady fell to the grass weeping, while the husband lunged forward to tackle the prophet off the small plot. Immediately he was stopped by an unseen force, a massive gust of wind that quickly blew him back and then vanished once the young man placed his hands back down to his sides. All of a sudden, the ground beneath the prophet exploded under his feet, knocking him into the air and right over the a small stone planter head first. The younger man fell back onto his petite wife, nearly knocking her in the head with his boots.

In front of their eyes, a young girl came crawling out of the tomb. Her body and clothing were all intact. The young couple, in a daze, grabbed the young girl, holding her tight and weeping for joy. The mother shouted "Angela!" They cried for a long time together. "I told you Jesus was real!" was all the prophet said. In the midst of the commotion, the young father turned to thank the prophet, only to find that he was gone. He was not seen ever again.

It was as if he was a stranger in a strange land, just passing through. Before going out to the graveyard, the young prophet had been preaching at a church in town. His message was about how miracles can really happen today. The majority of those in the service did not seem interested, but this young couple received the message, and their lives were forever changed. It was their faith that compelled the prophet to stop preaching about miracles and start showing how real God's power is.

Young Angela went on to live over twenty more years. The town wrote about this and many news channels followed up years later. Before long, those who experienced this great and mighty miracle passed on. In time, the entire town took on a whole new image and most people who had been raised from the dead eventually passed on through the natural course of life. After many years, this story was told as folklore by some attempting to undermine the power of God. There was only one problem—the media captured some of it live, and these files still remain in the county library under the direct care of Angela's daughter. You see, after Angela came back to life, she eventually got married and had a daughter before passing on. Angela's husband and daughter remain in that town to this day. Her husband, by the way, is the nephew to one of the men that had come back to life and lived nearly twelve more years.

> *"So I spoke this message, just as he told me. Suddenly as I spoke, there was a rattling noise all across the valley. The bones of each body came together and attached themselves as complete skeletons. Then as I watched, muscles and flesh formed over the bones. Then skin formed to cover their bodies, but they still had no breath in them. Then he said to me, 'Speak a prophetic message to the winds, son of man. Speak a prophetic message and say, "This is what the Sovereign Lord says: Come, O breath, from the four winds! Breathe into these dead bodies so they may live again."'"*
> *(Ezekiel 37:7-9).*

Paradise

"Will you receive Me this dark night? There is no one else but you, My friend, My equal. I need you this night to arise and be with Me. You are My loyal dove, a perfect partner for Me" (Song of Songs 5:2, TPT).

The crowds warred violently against Him. They were all one big unified angry mob wanting to kill Him and then turn on the rest of us. The roars of obscenity and disrespect for human regard would have run much deeper than it did, had it not been for the pain our bodies were feeling then. The ground below our hanging bodies were filled with blood pools, growing larger as the blood kept flowing out. How much fluid can a body really hold? We were about to find out soon.

"Shut up, you fools! Die!" The more defiant leader said to the one on the other side. "Had you not been a coward and come clean all of this would not have happened, now would it?" *This just didn't make any sense*, I thought. *Why is this happening? Why is it that Barabbas was let go and he was the one that had come up with the whole plan. He was the ringleader and now he was set free! There were three of us always together, always on the way to the next big heist, or fleeing to the next city to avoid taxes or the guards. Barabbas was the leader, not me or him. Why is this Man in the middle up here with us? What did He do that was so bad? All the witnesses were proven false and the prosecutions were not lining up.*

There was silence for moment and then I looked at the Man in the middle again. He was just staring out, looking up at the sky. The crowds of people continued yelling and shaking their fists at Him. They seemed to be angrier at Him more than they were at me or my partner on the other side of Him. We were the ones that stole the money and committed all the crimes. We hurt them a lot more than this Man in the middle ever could. What did He do that was so bad to them?

The blood flowed more as the sun beat down on us. Each of us fought harder and harder to breathe as our lungs began to collapse under the weight of our own bodies. The flies were tormenting. They could sense death was coming and were landing all over us. A few vultures rested high on an embankment just a short distance away, waiting for their next meal—us. At this point, the pain was so bad my mind started shutting down to avoid shock. Even now more scavengers were taking their spots, waiting for the right moment to attack our helpless bodies. There was nothing that anyone could do but just wait for us to die. The soldiers pushed back the crowds and even taunted them from time to time to keep the entertainment going. In my mind, there was just not much time left…or so I thought.

The Man in the middle looked directly at me. Those piercing eyes saw right through my soul and cut directly into my heart as if He knew what I would say next. "Look, I'm here because I deserve it, but you are innocent!" He blinked, tears flowing. "There is something totally different about You than us." The man on the other side cursed us both and then mocked the Man in the middle. Not me. I could feel in my heart something burning like a fire. What I felt when He looked at me was unlike anything I had ever experienced before. It was as if all the sounds of the crowds around us faded to silence and all the pain in my body ceased. I did not need any more proof. Indeed this was the Son of God! "Can I go with You when You die?" I asked. At this point I had nothing to lose. I didn't know why He would want me, but I had to ask because I believe He is the Answer. His response shocked me more than the nails in my hands. "This day, you will be with Me in My paradise!"

In time the roaring crowds began to slowly fade, my eyes began to flood with tears, except these were not normal tears. This water I never tasted before. I could feel pure and holy water flowing down over my body and into my soul. It was the Spirit of God washing all my hideous sins away. Forgiven! The pain began to fade dramatically as the sun dimmed in the light that was resting on the Man in the middle; Jesus is what they called Him. For a brief moment, there was only the two of us. I never saw a more beautiful light in all my life. The scavenger birds in the distance no longer scared me. *They can have this body*, I thought, *it is just a shell compared to what is living inside me now. The crowds... well, they were right. I deserve to die and so did that man on the other side. Jesus? No, He does not.*

The water and the blood began to spill more and more from Him. The water from that Man filled my body and the blood filled my heart. The passion—it exploded my life! I was dying on the outside, but I became alive on the inside. I began to feel more love than I could ever imagine for the world I once hated. I loved all those people more than life! I wish they could see Jesus the way I do now. They would not be saying and doing those things that hurt the heart of God.

One by one, we breathed our last. The man on the other side of Jesus, never once gave Jesus any credit, respect, or honor. As for me, just as the Messiah said, I found myself right in His arms in a whole new place. I saw my grandmother and my best friend. I saw my child who had died only minutes after birth, its once damaged body now perfect and completely whole. I felt no pain at all and I was completely clothed in clean garments with a totally new body. I will never forget those words, "This day, you will be with Me in My paradise"

"Then he said, 'Jesus, remember me when you come into your kingdom.' And Jesus replied, 'I assure you, today you will be with me in paradise'" (Luke 23:42-43).

The African Doctor

*"So the disciples went out, telling everyone they met to repent
of their sins and turn to God. And they cast out many demons
and healed many sick people, anointing them with olive oil"
(Mark 6:12-13).*

The medical doctor fell to the floor, knocking his surgery utensils over with him. The nurses raced to attend the doctor as he lay weeping on the dirty, blood-stained operating room floor. Moments later he appeared motionless. No one knew the cause of his fall, but there the doctor lay, lifeless in front of so many people. The room was packed with children and adults all being treated with HIV and AIDS. Many of these patients were return clients, barely getting the basic treatments for such a serious disease. Low budgets due to lack of funds were driving this little medical mission hut right into extinction. The doctor and workers knew that leaving was not an option and that a breakthrough was definitely on the horizon soon. Little did they know that so much was about to change in so little time. The locals were crying out to Jesus for miracles more and more. They were seeing how the facility was slowly dwindling down to bare minimum treatments, and medicine was so scarce that they all knew they could no longer turn to medical treatments alone.

After roughly twenty minutes laying on the floor without any motion a voice rang out, "I've seen enough!" It was the doctor. "Get my Bible!" He called out to the nurse. A young boy reached across the lines of waiting people and grabbed the doctor's Bible, handing it to the nurse. Just then a flash came from the boy's hand as he placed his hand back by his side. A surge of energy slammed into the young lad as if he had just plugged himself into a high voltage current. He fell forward onto some people standing in front of him and then onto the dirty floor and instantly the sores that had covered his body were gone! His mother leaped with joy as she saw her son healed right before her eyes. This young boy had contacted HIV through a blood transfusion. The doctor stood to his feet with the Bible in his hands. He turned to this Scripture and read it out loud two times.

> *"God gave Paul the power to perform unusual miracles. When handkerchiefs or aprons that had merely touched his skin were placed on sick people, they were healed of their diseases, and evil spirits were expelled" (Acts 19:11-12).*

With great boldness, the doctor took his surgical coat off, grabbed some cooking oil out of the kitchen, and poured it all over his coat. Cooking oil was dripping everywhere. "Your will, Lord. Your will be done," he said loudly as he threw the coat onto the crowds of people. As the coat passed over those in the front line, illnesses instantly vanished. One lady grew an eye right in her socket again. She had lost her eye years ago through a rebel raid in her community. She had been raped and that is how she contracted HIV, which had also disappeared instantly. Another man had a jaw bone and new teeth form inside his mouth! This man had fallen off a cliff years ago and landed on his face. If that hadn't been bad enough, he had also been on heavy drugs at the time and had received an infected needle. The effects of AIDS was gone too! One by one, people were healed as the coat was flung in the air over the crowds of sick people. The coat came to a sudden stop as it landed on about four children. All four of them were knocked to the floor like a bolt of lightning hit them. They laid there motionless for a moment, then one of the children crawled out from under the doctor's coat and the crowds looked with amazement at him and then the doctor. "What on earth!" a young lady who knew the boy shouted as she stood nearby gazing at what she had just witnessed. The crowd was in awe. This particular young boy was being treated for a very large tumor on his right ear. While under the white coat, the tumor fell off then disappeared into thin air. Another shouted," I can feel medicine in my body!" The other two had protruding stomachs that shrank back to normal size. They were starving, yet on this day God came down to feed the hungry with a food directly from heaven.

People all around were perplexed and in awe at what God was doing through this doctor's coat. As people got close to the coat, some fell over as if they fainted; others screamed and shouted that they could feel the power of God moving through their bodies. Some began to dance because legs grew back. One man jumped up out of the crowds and shouted that his arm had just come to life again. Even the locals testified that he had been born with a limp arm and had not used it once since birth. Later his mother came by the facility with actual papers documenting the birth deformity.

Before long, news spread quickly in the streets that an amazing thing was happening in the little medical mission. The crowds grew so fast that the "miracle cloth" and the doctor were moved outside on the streets. As people walked by, some were knocked to the ground and others were deemed "unconscious" in their vehicles. The doctor placed his hands on one after the next until all in that village were healed. When this miraculous intervention was over, the doctor directed the crowds to repent and believe in Jesus Christ.

Strangely enough, the government authorities came and arrested this doctor for "disorderly conduct" and he was sentenced to three years in prison. While in prison he saw hundreds of people saved, healed, and delivered. The more they persecuted him the more anointing occurred around him. Few around him even knew his name; they just called him "the doctor." While in prison, even the guards respected him enough to bend some rules from time to time. He soon died a martyr for Jesus Christ right there in that old, concrete African cell. Inmates told many stories how this man would preach for hours on end through his little cement cell.

One day, the prison authorities found him dead, asleep in his bed with a smile on his face. The cell the doctor lived in has been marked a "holy cell" by the prisoners, being that everyone who has taken that cell since has had divine encounters at night as they slept, and during the day as they sit. Cell guards have more than once required this cell to be opened and all the contents seized because they have witnessed another person in this one-person cell talking or eating meals with the cell's current occupant. Some said they have seen angels or people standing right next to the inmates. Others once testified to the chief supervisor that there was a doctor working on a sick inmate in that cell. All this said, the records in this prison remain true that there has never been more than one person assigned to that cell at a time.

As for the doctor's jacket, it still sits in the abandoned medical mission storefront. People in the town say that it continues to drip oil, and when people get near the hems of this garment, it is still healing sickness and infirmities of every kind. Some have come from all over parts of the world to witness this amazing phenomenon.

> *"Just then a woman who had suffered for twelve years with constant bleeding came up behind him. She touched the fringe of his robe, for she thought, 'If I can just touch his robe, I will be healed.' Jesus turned around, and when he saw her he said, 'Daughter, be encouraged! Your faith has made you well.' And the woman was healed at that moment" (Matthew 9:20-22).*

The Father's Door

"There is more than enough room in my Father's home. If this were not so, would I have told you that I am going to prepare a place for you?" (John 14:2).

I stepped cautiously inside the gigantic entryway; peeking this way and that for signs of movement. To my amazement there was nobody present inside this extremely large building. I was taken aback by the immaculate décor that lined every section of the edifice. In some areas of the floor, golden images glistened throughout. This was a transparent gold not seen before on earth. One could notice their reflection in it, yet at the same time look into it and right through the particles all at once. All three distinct qualities resonated in every area of the gold. The other flooring sections had unimaginable tiles as thick as solid rock and crafted in the finest detail on earth. The carpeted areas were so soft that I felt like I was floating on designer rugs as I walked gently across them. The walls were spotless and the exquisite curtains looked as if they weighed a ton.

I continued walking a bit closer to a door at the end of the hall that was open and well lit. Masterpiece artwork lined the halls, each illustrating a specified moment in time. Every gem imaginable gleamed through the walls of this giant facility. To think I could possibly be alone was an understatement. Every step of the way filled more and more of my heart with an extravagant love and a peace unlike anything I had ever felt before. I thought I understood peace, but this was a whole new beginning for me. The closer I got to the door at the end of the immaculate hall, the more I felt like bursting on the inside. My inner being was exploding with an overwhelming presence.

As I finally reached the room at the end, I walked through the entryway and closed the door behind me. I wandered into the dwelling, my curiosity now peaked. Door after door lined the hallway of the immense mansion leading up to a single entryway. The previous hall led to a single door to get where I was currently standing. Indeed, there was only one door to get here. One way in and one way out and when I stepped through the framing, it immediately felt like the divine Spirit of God hovered near. In this new area I was standing in, there were too many doors to count and too many to visit. This particular area showed many colors and rainbows all through the air. Flashes of brilliant light came out of nowhere and gently floated through the room. There was life resonating through those beams of light, as if someone or something knew I was standing there. From time to time, one "orb" looking creature would float right over my head or near my body. Instantly I felt life and love. This experience was like a dead battery being recharged instantly to full capacity, ready to function again. Energy emanated from this room of many colors. At every glance, colors known and unknown skimmed throughout the atmosphere, just like a ballerina dancing across the floor. Sometimes it was as if the different light beams were communicating and somehow dancing with each other. All of the light functioned in complete unity toward one another and also highly respected my presence. *Maybe they were all expecting me*, I thought over and over again. The peace of God reigned supreme in the corridor; there was no strife, quarreling, or fear. Most assuredly, I had stepped into a new dimension of time, not found on earth. It was a place where angels lived in perfect harmony. The "orb" appearances were illuminations of angelic hosts moving throughout the room. There must have been thousands of them if one could actually see them all in number.

One door down on the other end of the room looked as if it were created just for me. I was drawn to it and began to walk toward it. This door made me feel more at home the closer I came to it. The brilliant sparkling finish was a kind not of this earth. The sparkles had life within them. One could feel life moving through the light as if different parts of the light were communicating with each other and attempting to communicate with me. Although this door had appeared to have been made centuries ago, it had never faded through time. It somehow took on more character but did not lesson or tarnish. The wood on this door was like it never died but continued to live even though it had been cut and created by hand. Brilliance shined through the texture like the sun shines in the noon day, piercing all the way through the summer clouds. There was not a lock on the door, or even a handle; there was no need for one. If you couldn't walk through the door, it wouldn't matter anyway, because there were so many other places to venture into inside the mansion. Besides that, you just knew in your heart whether you should or should not do anything. As I drew near the door, it opened as if a mother was awaiting the arrival of her lost child. This type of anticipation and excitement within the atmosphere was awe inspiring. I felt a subtle wind brush across my body that felt like a warm breeze on a hot summer's day underneath a large shady tree; it felt safe and relaxing.

Through this door was a new dimension of creativity that dazzled my heart as I saw colors never yet described by the human mind. At every angle the colors seemed to shift into an endless array of artistic designs. Once again, the light was living. The ceiling reached as high as the eye could possibly envision, structured by lining after lining of the purest form of crystallized glass images. For a person to create just one section of this room would appear to take a lifetime commitment.

For a moment I felt ashamed to be standing in such a place like this. I started to back out of the doorway for fear that my presence would not be welcomed in such a beautiful dwelling. This was a perfectly created structure with now an imperfect person standing within. The door behind me remained open should I desire to leave the room, yet I knew in my heart that I could never turn back into that hallway the same way I came in. The energy in the room was welcoming and pure, wanting me to stay more than I wanted to leave.

After a moment I heard a voice say, "Come here, My son." The voice was just like the sound of many crystal chimes singing in the wind. It was strong enough to shatter any substance, yet as gentle as a lion with her newborn cubs. The Lord's voice had come from the other side of the room. As I turned to Him, He asked with a big smile, "Do you like this room?" I didn't know what to say, my heart still staggering to be in a paradise like this. As the Lord moved in my direction, glorious clouds of many dimensions, designs, and colors were floating at His feet. A beautiful fragrance was released into the air as He walked and it started to melt my heart. Memories of self-pity, regret, and discouragement dissipated as a vapor in the air. I took my shoes off and bowed to the floor, tears streaming down my face. The flooring definitely wasn't carpet found in a store. It was as thick as grizzly bear fur, and as clean as the mountain streams. As if this were not amazing enough the floor was as soft as a newborn baby's skin. Again, even the floor seemed to move with me as I walked, as though it was actually attempting to communicate with me. The Spirit brought energetic power to everything around us.

The Lord bent down next to me, took the hem of His robe, and washed my dirty, stained feet. "My son, I remember when you got these stains on your feet," He said, grinning as He looked up at me.

He stuck out his hand toward mine. I grasped His hand and He lifted me to my feet. He picked me up and held me like a little child safe and warm on a cold winter night. "Why so many rooms?" was all I could ask. "The rooms," He said in a soft voice, "represent who I am. Each room was crafted with just as much creativity as the next one; not a single error was made and no two are the same. A different dimension of the power of My love for all people is shown by each distinct room. I made this one for you and all who want to know my creativity in ways not understood by the human mind. When I said you would do greater things, I meant it, but these greater things must start in this room and no other. Creativity is only forged through the power of My love."

"Why this room?" I asked.

"Because this room reveals the heart of intimacy of My Father toward His children," He answered. "My creativity only comes through spending time with Me—building a deep relationship."

At that moment, we were still in the room but the atmosphere changed slightly, I felt a sense of profound love and pure peace. Jesus put me on His lap as He sat firm on His golden throne. There was a scepter near His right hand. The handle had a crystal-green tint. He gazed into my eyes with all the love and adoration of a mother looking at her newborn baby. After giving me a big hug, He gently rubbed my back, running His fingers through my hair and even tracing around my face. Purity and love could be felt in His touch. Then He said with a smile, "Take off, run and hide!" Not knowing what to do, I did what He said and ran as fast as I could, hiding behind a sword held by the hand of an angel. I chuckled to myself at the oddity of the game—playing hide and seek with an omnipresent God! Of course, the Lord found me in no time. We laughed together as we played and then He put His arm around my shoulders like a proud father. As time went by it all began to sink deep within my soul.

"So you have not received a spirit that makes you fearful slaves. Instead, you received God's Spirit when he adopted you as his own children. Now we call him, 'Abba, Father.'" (Romans 8:15).

My Heavenly Father was solely focused on me! All He wanted to do was spend time with me. This intensely personal time with the Lord just flew by. Often, He would embrace me in His arms. Most amazingly, the Lord actually took a few moments and showed some stylish, yet discreet, dance moves. Yes, we actually danced with each other as a father would celebrate with his son who has just became an adult. I think it was more fun for the Lord to teach me the new steps as more times than counted, I would step on His feet. His mercy and grace showed through His face as He would throw his head back and laugh with me, love and joy streaming from His eyes. There was no fear in the room, because He did not care what mistakes I made, He just wanted to be with me. The angels stood around every wall of this room, guarding it with their swords and golden shields. Every weapon was hand crafted out of the finest gold and was made specifically for that particular angel. Absolutely nothing in this entire facility was mass produced or generic in style.

After a while He placed me on His shoulders and walked me to the entrance door. Once at the entrance, He slipped me down from His shoulders and placed a jar of wine in my hands, saying "This is not earthly wine, My son." Looking me directly in the eyes, He said, "This is a jar filled with My intimacy for My children." There was silence for a brief moment. "Come back anytime you want, but as you leave each time, go and spread this wine-oil upon the hearts of every wounded, battered, strife-driven, and weary child of God you find. In My presence there is peace and nothing is impossible for Me. Lead them down the same hall that you came in today. Teach My children to desire My intimacy more than anything else in this world." And with that, He told me He loved me and then bent down and kissed my forehead. "Go in My peace, My love, and My joy."

Remember, The Father's Door is always open and never shut. There are no locks on this door, meaning that you are always welcome. The Lord wants to spend personal time with you. He has set all other plans aside, just to be near His children today. In fact, He is more than willing to change His plans, just to be with you.

> *"Going over to him, the Samaritan soothed his wounds with olive oil and wine and bandaged them. Then he put the man on his own donkey and took him to an inn, where he took care of him" (Luke 10:34).*

Dirty Feet on Golden Floors

"We will dance in the high place of the sky. Yes, on the mountains of fragrant spice! Forever we shall be united as One!" (Song of Songs 8:14, TPT).

Gold glistened in the young boy's wide open eyes as he peered up the intimidating stairwell. From the top all the way to the bottom, the purest of gold gleamed across the entryway of this towering palace. These steps were a rare set, not at all common. The handrails were built right into the steps as one piece.

The young boy thought for a moment, *Should I go? Is this really real? Can I climb these steps?* He climbed up on the first step, grabbing the railing with his left hand. Then he walked up about 10 golden and perfectly spotless steps. At that moment, the intricate structure curved off to the left.

At the pivoting point, there were flaming golden fires on both sides of the golden steps that led up to a splendid room above. Hesitant to continue, the young boy took a deep breath, not sure of what would transpire as his body came into contact with the golden flames. One more step and then he placed a hand on the handrail. Another step and then another hand on the rail. Each step drawing him closer to the almighty presence of God. He was speechless, to say the least!

The golden flames danced back and forth, even bowing toward the heavens in unison. It was a very eloquent feeling, as if the flames were touching the young man's soul while they danced in the mighty strength of God. The experience was out of this world, as if he were free falling with perfect gentle peace.

The boy got almost to the top of the steps and out came Jesus with a smile. He stood right at the entryway and was excited to see the young, intimidated lad. He stood there dressed in a very simple outfit, yet at the same time the material was so fine that no normal machine could have manufactured it. The Lord turned around and led the young boy into the extremely large dwelling. The room had several shades of gold within. The texture, fixtures, and structures were all purely solid gold, and was so clean, a fingerprint could not be found anywhere.

The floor was what grabbed the young boy's attention. There was a swirling effect in its very composition, as if you could see a crystal river of glass mixed right into the golden color, with a hint of pearl. The floor itself remained constant, but underneath the top coat of this floor was actually a moving river of crystal clear water from one end to the other. Walking on this floor appeared as if one were walking on a crystal glassy-golden sea. You could look through the solid shell of it, yet also see the momentum of life moving underneath. Jesus looked at the young boy and said, "What can I tell you?" *Oh!* The youngster thought as he suddenly looked down, noticing his feet. *My sandals and feet are all dirty*, the young boy thought. At that precise moment, the Lord, in His extravagant clothing, bent down and began to wash and dry the boy's feet. The dirt lay there on the golden floor.

The young boy was about to respond to the embarrassment of the dirt from his feet, now soiling the Lord's extravagant floor. However, Jesus went ahead and brought up the conversation.

"The dirt is fine." Jesus said, "That dirt reminds Me of how you used to be before you accepted Me as your Savior. You are not dirty on the inside any longer." His eyes were radiant, "I embrace who you are now;

a young man who has been made clean." Jesus leaned toward the young boy and looked him straight in his face, eye to eye, and He said with a serious, yet blissful demeanor. "I just want to be with you."

"And I am convinced that nothing can ever separate us from God's love. Neither death nor life, neither angels nor demons, neither our fears for today nor our worries about tomorrow—not even the powers of hell can separate us from God's love. No power in the sky above or in the earth below—indeed, nothing in all creation will ever be able to separate us from the love of God that is revealed in Christ Jesus our Lord" (Romans 8:38-39).

About the Author

Thank you so much for taking the time to read this book. I hope you enjoyed it! There is something else I would like you to read, and it will only take a moment of your time. You see, I am alive today because Jesus changed my life!

By the time I was two years old, I was given only six months to live due to a life-threatening blood disorder. It was at this time that my parents took me for prayer at their home church, calling on the name of the Lord. Shortly after this prayer, God intervened, and I was divinely healed just two weeks later. Jesus changed my life!

One afternoon in 1992, just three weeks before my high school graduation, I died of a drug overdose. This one event caused me to see Jesus face-to-face and also witness my dead, lifeless body down on earth. Through this incredible encounter I was brought back to life and instantly set free from drugs. Several weeks later, I gave my heart to the Lord in a county jail cell late on a Friday night. It was there that God called me by name and set me free from alcohol. Within one year, God sent me to Bible college where I met my wonderful wife, Cathy.

In my freshman year of college I was placed in remedial English due to my lack of skill in reading and writing. I certainly was not college material back then, but once, again God had special plans.

In 1999 I had another encounter with God that lasted nearly two and a half hours. This is when the Lord imparted to me the ability to prophesy and gave me the anointing to write. This is when the passion for creative media all began.

In the year 2000, I got involved with publishing, often working late evening hours to volunteer with media efforts behind the scenes. In 2005, I started writing a small, encouraging e-mail to five people each week. (I think two or three of the people did not even care to read them!) This small beginning was discouraging, but God told me to keep on writing. I began writing on an international scale in 2008 and have continued to do so. Depending on what venues accept these writings God gives me, they are sent to viewers worldwide.

Not only did the Lord implant in me a desire to prophesy and write, He also put within me a longing for knowledge. After earning a bachelor of arts degree in Bible Studies from Central Bible College in Springfield, Missouri, I continued my studies at Freedom Seminary in Rogers, Arkansas. There I received my master's degree and doctorate in Christian education, earning the status of summa cum laude and President's honor roll. Once again, Jesus changed my life!

These are some of the many reasons 5 Fold Media, LLC was founded. We are passionate about creative media and seeing lives changed for Jesus. God broke my addictions and then took my inability to write and turned it into a promising opportunity to touch the world for Him. God has changed my life!

God bless,
Andy Sanders

If you have received any insight, encouragement, or healing from the writings in this book, I would love to hear from you! Contact me at andy@5foldmedia.com.

Music by Cathy Sanders
All CDs $10.00 each
Downloadable full-length CDs for only $6.00 each!
Visit www.5foldmedia-store.com

God of Breakthrough
Cathy's newest CD carries a fresh anointing and expectancy of God's touch as you experience the presence of God through spontaneous LIVE worship!

Fire by Night
This CD is marked by the presence of the Lord as well as a creative story of life and faith. It includes many different styles from urban to worship.

I Choose Your Ways
Cathy's first CD is filled with touching songs that were written from her personal life experiences. Join the many lives that have been touched by the messages in these songs.

More Titles by 5 Fold Media

The Most Amazing Song of All
by Brian Simmons
ISBN: 978-1-936578-03-0
$9.00

Breathtaking and beautiful, we see the Shulamite journey unveiled in this anointed allegory. It becomes a journey that not only describes the divine parable penned by Solomon, but a journey that every longing lover of Jesus will find as his or her very own.

In this new Passion Translation™, the translator uses the language of the heart based on a passion for love to translate the book from Hebrew to English.

Daddy, If You Only Knew
by Steve & Lennette Deal
ISBN: 978-0-9825775-0-9
$15.00

America has vastly become a fatherless nation. Now the children's voices uncut, unedited, and sometimes harsh are revealed regarding their relationships, or lack thereof, with their fathers. This book compiles some of their letters pouring out their hearts to their fathers, known and unknown.

"You will experience, from the pens of these children, their pain and the longing to be loved, nurtured, and taught by their Father."
- Abraham Brown,
Founder, Owner, Abe Brown Ministries

Visit www.5foldmedia.com to sign up for **5 Fold Media's FREE email updates.** You will get notices of our new releases, sales, and special events such as book signings and media conferences.

5 Fold Media, LLC is a Christ-centered media company. Our desire is to produce lasting fruit in writing, music, art, and creative gifts.

"To Establish and Reveal"
For more information visit:
www.5foldmedia.com

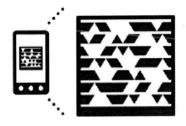

Use your mobile device to scan the tag above and visit our website.
Get the free app: http://gettag.mobi

CPSIA information can be obtained at www.ICGtesting.com
Printed in the USA
BVOW041517251111

276834BV00001B/5/P